INTO

HIS

PRESENCE

— INTO —

HIS

PRESENCE

HOW *TO* FIND *THE* ULTIMATE TREASURE

Dr. Francis Sizer

DESTINY IMAGE® PUBLISHERS, INC.
P.O. Box 310, Shippensburg, PA 17257-0310

"Speaking to the Purposes of God for this Generation
and for the Generations to Come."

This book and all other Destiny Image, Revival Press, Mercy Place, Fresh Bread, Destiny Image Fiction, and Treasure House books are available at Christian bookstores and distributors worldwide.

For a U.S. bookstore nearest you, call 1-800-722-6774. For more information on foreign distributors, call 717-532-3040. Or reach us on the Internet: www.destiny-image.com

ISBN 10: 0-7684-2487-9
ISBN 13: 978-0-7684-2487-4

For Worldwide Distribution, Printed in the U.S.A.

1 2 3 4 5 6 7 8 9 10 11 / 09 08 07

DEDICATIONS

This book is dedicated to my late, loving father, James J. Sizer Sr., who passed on to me a measure of his wisdom and discernment and to my kind mother, Mary T. Sizer, who taught me the meaning of love and forgiveness. To both of them I owe my formation from the past. I dedicate this book, likewise, to my beautiful wife, Eileen, who walks beside me closer than any in the present. And finally, I dedicate this book to my gifted son, Joshua, who gives me a hope and a promise for the future.

ACKNOWLEDGEMENTS

I'd like to acknowledge Nancy Rankin Moffitt together with her loving husband George, their daughter, Nancy Ann, and their late brother in the Lord, Nick. This Christian family exemplifies Paul's words to the Thessalonians, *"We continually remember before our God and Father your work produced by faith, your labor prompted by love, and your endurance inspired by hope in our Lord Jesus Christ."* (1Thess. 1:2-3).

I'd like to acknowledge my very dear friends John and Rose Moon, Richard and Janet Foster, Dennis and Carolyn Zaverl, Art and Kim Palacas, Tom and Sue Yancy, and Jim and Kathy Healy.

Likewise, thanks go out to my late father-in-law, Peter Lynch, Jr. for his daily prayers for the publication of **Into His Presence** as well as all the prayers of family and loved ones, in particular, Maria Buzzi. Finally, my gratitude goes out to Pastor Hong, Wonsun Bang, and Kevin for the artistic illustrations he provided and to all my Korean friends in Seoul.

CONTENTS

CONTENTS

CONTENTS

PART ONE
STEPPING INTO GOD

CHAPTER ONE

THE UNDENIABLE CALL

"This one is to be the priest," said the wiry, old Irish woman without hesitation. All eight of us children lined up like toy soldiers at attention. Her long, thin finger pointed at me as if she knew something none of us others knew. She was hired by my mother to clean the house, but Mary Smeddy was always larger than life to us children. We were frightened of her. I recall one time sliding down the banister just to avoid stepping on her newly polished steps. She was from the old school of thought. She valued authority and obedience above sensitivity to the feelings of others. Her word ruled.

We weren't rich as a family, but my mother needed help. If my memory serves me right, my mother was either busy with morning sickness during a pregnancy, or she was carrying a bundle of clothes to the laundry room to be washed or ironed. Cleaning the huge six-bedroom suburban house was daunting when raising multiple children with others on the way.

In any event, this is where Mary Smeddy stepped into the picture. She commanded our respect. Prophecy or not, the word came to pass. I did become the priest. As a high school graduate, I looked forward to life in college pursuing a secular career. This apparently was not to be. Something kept nagging inside me to become a priest. The thought and feeling just wouldn't go away. As much as I would try to dismiss it, it returned with a growing persistence.

My father then talked to me about my future. He said, "Frank, you could be whatever you want to be, and I'm sure you would be a success. But please consider becoming a priest before you do anything else." Those words stuck in my mind. My family was a deeply devout and prayerful one. Being devout and prayerful is one thing, but being obsessed with God was quite another.

No matter what career I would investigate, I would see His face. As I thought of pursuing a law career, I rationalized that I could practice constitutional law by defending the rights and values with biblical principles. As I considered becoming a physician bringing healing to the body, all I could see was the heart of Father God calling me closer. Although there is obvious value and excellence to these professions, God seemed to be calling me to another path. While it may have seemed that I entered seminary in part to please my earthly father, it was really the call of my heavenly Father that I was answering.

My head and my heart were in conflict. I could not seem to get it together. My head wanted to run down the road of success, while my heart turned toward Jesus not knowing where that path would lead. I found myself at a fork in the road of my life. The path of professional security seemed like a sure thing, while the path following God seemed nebulous. The future down this path was not well defined. It would require walking blindly, trusting that God would show me the way.

The Hound of Heaven

As the summer wore on before college, the decision to enter the seminary loomed over me. It was as if I couldn't escape His beckoning call. Until I surrendered to the issues of my heart, I would have no peace. No rest would come back to my soul until I turned over my will to His personal invitation, "Come closer." The words of poet Francis Thompson spring to mind in his brilliant, poetic work *The Hound of Heaven.*

> *I fled Him, down the nights and down the days;*
> *I fled Him, down the arches of the years;*
> *I fled Him, down the labyrinthine ways*
> *Of my own mind; and in the midst of tears*
> *I hid from Him…*

The genius of Francis Thompson, a tortured soul, mad and alcoholic, puts its finger upon the very essence of God's desire to pierce our life. Happiness comes in following hard after Him; misery comes in the denial. G. K. Chesterton wrote that the primary point of the genius of Thompson comes in the awakening of the

"Domini canes," (Dogs of God). This implies that the hunt for the souls of men is up once more. It signaled a return to personal religion where God cares about each and every soul, ready to pursue them until they might succumb. Religion, when left unattended, degrades into sterile ritual. Religion, as an end in itself, impersonalizes both humanity and God. However, those who dare pay heed to the gnawing, beating call of the Hound of Heaven find themselves on a path like Job and Jonah before them. Like David in Psalm 139 they shout out, *"Where can we run from Your Spirit?"*

I believe there are tens of thousands like me who hear the gnawing, beating call, who listen with the ear of their soul to the very heartbeat of God. Those with their hand on the pulse of their life, with His blood coursing through their veins, will witness to the truth that their life is not their own. They will echo with me that their life is owned by another greater than they are. They will acknowledge that their will to be and to do is an answer to His will for them. His generally gentle yet persistent call is always there. He is ever bidding us to come. He is ever wooing us into deeper relationship.

It is ironic that sometimes we think we are pursuing God when what is really happening is that **God is pursuing us**. God has released the chase to be upon us. The Hounds of Heaven are unleashed. His love and concern for us is so compelling that He desires that *"not one of us perish"* (John 3:16). For *"You did not chose Me, I chose you"* (John 15:16).

A Personal Encounter

In 1966, I entered the Catholic seminary for eight years of formation as a priest. The seminary model at that time could be likened to a type of monastic life with high precedence given to silence and contemplation. The practice of the presence of God through silence and meditation encouraged a life built upon prayer. This type of prayer life helped create a heartfelt desire for God. This lifestyle came at a time in our society when a revolution occurred in values and morals. Noise, loud rock music, and the proliferation of television, movies, drugs, and alcohol filled the human soul. For most the idea of encountering silence seemed uncomfortable and even agitating.

Every venerable saint of the ages teaches the need to empty from distraction in order to hear and fellowship with God. Jesus often went off alone to pray. The noise of the world can easily distract us from communicating with God. My formation in the seminary gave me the tools for creating a well inside me for the Lord.

In 1966, I won a prestigious scholarship to study in Rome, Italy for the next ten years. I am sure this would have led me on a different path. It certainly would have led to an education in the cradle of the Vatican. I decided to decline the honor since I wanted to serve as a parish priest. A parish priest is essentially one who works as a curet. In his work *Care of the Soul*, Thomas Moore, a former monk, rightly describes the role of the parish priest as one who has spiritual charge over those souls living within the boundaries of his church. *Curet* meant "charge" as well as "care." He was to tend the soul in times of birth, illness, marriage, crisis, and death. The priest is not there at these important moments to fix or cure but rather to be a presence of God in these moments in time. This type of presence is what appealed to me.

Those long years in the local seminary taught me much about theology and about the Scriptures. More importantly, I was formed inside and outside as a representative of the Church. Ordination came in 1974 at the beautiful basilica in Philadelphia. My work in ministry as a priest was about to begin.

At my first church, I could talk about Jesus, but I didn't know Jesus. The work I did in my ministry was good, but things were not happening like they did in the Book of the Acts of the Apostles.

This discrepancy between reality and ideal created a nagging tension. *There must be more to ministry*, I thought. Once again that nagging feeling tugged at my soul. It wouldn't go away. As much as I tried to fit in with the normal duties of priesthood, it just wouldn't work. I could not make the desire for *more* go away. I wanted miracles in my life. I had to have the real thing. Nothing else would bring contentment. This great dissatisfaction could only be satisfied with more of Jesus.

My life came to a place of great need. Thank God when one comes to a place of need. While I was weeping and travailing for God, something happened. I had no great vision or appearance from Heaven that night, but what happened occurred within me. God's reassurance and peace dwelt in me. I knew before anything took place that something was about to change in my life. And it did.

A God experience like the one I just outlined is familiar territory to the very many who have had spiritual awakenings. A common thread is woven in the pattern of all our stories. Namely, at a point of desperation and need, we can no longer continue in the status quo. We need something more, but it is outside our grasp. Our flesh, our works, our talent, and our abilities cannot create it. It demands a supernatural encounter from God. During moments like these, when anything good seems out of our reach, a way is made for God to reach inside of us. It is under these conditions, that God's manifested presence touches us.

David knew what life was like both with God and without God. He knew what life was like when he walked close to the Lord. He also knew what life was like when he walked in sin and despair. He knew that his flesh was weak, and he remembered the strength from God's presence.

This is why David would write:

Create in me a pure heart, O God, and renew a steadfast spirit within me. Do not cast me from Your presence or take Your Holy Spirit from me. Restore to me the joy of Your salvation and grant me a willing spirit, to sustain me (Psalm 51:10-12).

David realized that when he walked without the presence of God, numerous troubles and sin followed. He realized as king that it was futile to rule without God's presence. King Saul, David's predecessor, ruled without deference to the presence of God. One remembers Saul left the Ark of God at Abinadab's house where it was left following the defeat of the Israelite army at Beth Shemesh. The leaders and troops had lost their sense of awe for God. They no longer walked in fear of the Lord. The Ark itself was mishandled and mistreated.

When Saul killed himself, one of David's first acts as king was to go seek out the Ark of God. He knew the vital importance of walking in the presence of God. He had entered into God's presence many times, and he knew as king of a nation, that God's presence must be in the midst of the people. David's hope for Israel was in bringing back the Ark of God's presence. David's hope was not in more government, more social programs, more education, or more gun control for Jerusalem. As his heart was a heart for God, he wanted the entire city to have a heart for God. David did not hesitate to pursue the Ark of God.

David took his troops to the house of Abinadab in Kiriath Jearim where it had been for 20 years. *"Let us bring the Ark of God back to us, for we did not inquire of it during the reign of Saul"* (1 Chron. 13:3). David had a heart for God. The key to David's life was not that he saw himself as holy. He knew his sin all too well. The key to David was his heart. David sought after God. Even when David failed to heed the directives of God Almighty, and sin visited him as a result, God was still there. He learned from his sin and grew in his obedience.

As David initially tried to bring back the Ark to Jerusalem, he did not treat it with the respect it was due. The fear of the Lord was not upon David. Uzzah, one of David's servants, foolishly handled and touched the Ark. David learned from his own disobedience. The Bible says, *"Uzzah reached out and took hold of the Ark of God, because the oxen stumbled. The Lord's anger burned against Uzzah because of his irreverent act; therefore God struck him down and he died there beside the Ark of God"* (2 Sam. 6:6-7). The second time, some months later, David again tried to bring back the Ark to Jerusalem. This time he was successful, because he acknowledged God's directives and walked with the fear of the Lord.

We need a healthy fear of the Lord because it is the beginning of wisdom (see Prov. 1:17). Wisdom, unlike knowledge, gives us God's approach to things. If one ever has the awesome opportunity to be in the tangible presence of the Lord, one intuitively knows to keep hands off. When God shows up in His manifested presence, and there are no more words spoken, no more songs sung, no more rituals carried out.

God's presence demands that one be humbled and silent before Him. As soon as flesh gets in the way, the glory of God lifts because His glory will share the spotlight with no man.

I recall a service in a church during which the manifested presence of God showed up. When this occurred it was like a cloud of His evident presence literally moved in. All sensitive to the things of the Spirit were aware of the change in the room. Things were no longer the same as usual. A thick, tangible presence was there when just a few moments ago it wasn't. It was like experiencing the guest of honor entering the room. One knew a special person was there without even turning around to see Him. As the thickness increased, the emotions were overwhelming feelings of love, unworthiness, transcendence, and immanence.

As the worship of the people continued without music, the cries of the people could be heard. God was touching His people with repentance. People began to experience "oil" in their hands. Others were experiencing "gold dust" all over their bodies. The pastor asked me what we should do about these phenomena. I simply said we were to thank God for them.

They seemed to be recognizable signs of His manifested presence. We were not so much drawn to the attention of the signs and wonders, but rather drawn to the attention of Him. As wonderful as the signs and wonders were, they were still signs that simply pointed to His presence.

The Book of Hebrews

The book of Hebrews has impacted my life more than any other book of the Bible. Being ordained as a Roman

Catholic priest made me curious about the meaning of the priesthood of Jesus as the fulfillment of the Old Testament sacrificial priesthood. The priesthood of Jesus must be seen against the backdrop of the Old Testament priesthood.

Deuteronomy 33:8-10 gives a description of the three essential functions of the priesthood of the Old Testament. The people of Israel went to the priest of the sanctuary: (1) to consult God for answers to problems they had; (2) to receive teaching from the Torah or Law of God; and (3) to offer sacrifice to God for sin. The first two duties were eventually passed over to the prophet and scribe respectively, while the third duty remained the essential mark of the Levitical priesthood. This third duty describes the quintessential role of the Lord Jesus wherein He is the Lamb of God.

I say this book of the Bible has special importance to me because I spent eight years of my younger life in preparation for ordination to the Catholic priesthood, and subsequently, over eight more years in ministry as a Catholic priest. During those years, I was influenced by a number of individuals and events. One individual and event I recall redirected the course of my life.

I was speaking in Washington, DC at a national conclave of Full Gospel businessmen. While at the convention, I was having breakfast with the group's president, Demos Shakarian, and a few of its national leaders. They were all Protestant men who were earnestly trying to understand the nature of the Catholic priesthood. They asked me numerous questions about the Mass, confession, and the Vatican. I did my very best in answering these men; however, I could readily perceive my answers to their questions were not hitting home. In the midst of this polite exchange, an elderly lady, impeccably dressed, came over to my table. She excused herself for the interruption, and simply said, "The answer is in the curtain." She then disappeared as quickly as she came. To this day I believe she was an angel.

Later in the day I looked up references to the word *curtain*, and came upon the Book of Hebrews. What I was about to read would forever change the course of my life.

Therefore, brothers, since we have confidence to enter into the Most Holy Place by the blood of Jesus, by a new and living way opened for us through the curtain, that is, His body...let us draw near (Hebrews 10:19-20).

As I read this passage, the revelation from God jumped off the page at me. I recalled that the curtain of the Temple was torn asunder at the very moment Jesus died on the cross. The death of Jesus made possible the dedication of the new sanctuary and opened a new and better way into the very presence of God through the veil or curtain of His flesh.

God was showing me that through Jesus, the one High Priest, all now have access to God without the need for any other intermediary. Until this time, the people needed an earthly priest to act as their intermediary between God and man. They needed someone to offer sin offerings to God in their behalf. I now could see clearly that Jesus came as priest to end the need for any more sacrifice for sin. His death is sufficient once for all.

All born out of His death are justified and sanctified in His blood. This is precisely why the classic "kingdom of priests" text from Exodus 19:6 finds its way into the New Testament: *"You are a chosen race, a royal priesthood, a holy nation, a people belonging to God"* (1 Pet. 2:9).

The fulfillment of the function of priests concluded and culminated with the offering of the one, true High Priest. The holiness of the people of God is based on that one perfect offering.   To better understand the meaning of the word "curtain" or "veil," one must understand the division within the Tabernacle and later in the Temple. Hebrews 9 describes the division of the Tabernacle in part with its Holy Place and its Holy of Holies. The curtain or veil divided these two sections. The priests entered habitually into the Holy Place to perform their ritual acts of worship. None would venture into the Holy of Holies except the high priest, and that occasion would only occur once a year. The veil then represented a separation between God and man.

The Most High God dwelt in the Holy of Holies. Love for God calls the sinner near in the Holy Place while righteousness would hold him back from entering into God's presence in the Holy of Holies.

The Tabernacle of Moses was so constructed after the heavenly pattern to bring forth one important truth. That truth is that a new and perfect way is opened for us who desire to enter into the presence of God. The Tabernacle and its furnishings provided a way for coming into the presence of God in the Old Testament times.

Now the new and perfect way is opened for us in Jesus who walked through the furnishings of the Tabernacle. He becomes our Altar of Sacrifice, our Laver of cleansing, our Table of Showbread, our Lampstand, our Altar of Incense, our Mercy Seat, and our Ark of the Covenant.

Our God was wrestling with me again. Here I was speaking at national conventions. I was giving frequent retreats to priests and nuns from many different orders. I was sought out as a speaker. My home church couldn't have been better. Our healing service was drawing thousands of people to its gatherings. Things were going great, yet God decided to pursue me once again. The Hound of Heaven seemed to want more. He was revealing truth to me in the Bible. He revealed truth about His church, and truth about Him being the priest.

If I thought for a moment I could ignore His voice because I was comfortable with my station in life, I was mistaken. The voice of God roared in my soul "Jesus came not to start a new priesthood of sacrifice, but to end the need for priesthood because of His sacrifice once for all." God was once again pulling me toward Himself.

God is always pulling on us, tugging on us to move ever closer to Him. He draws us into deeper relationship with

Him. God is never satisfied with where we find ourselves right now. He eggs us onward to a more challenging and richer walk with Him.

God invites you to follow the walk to intimacy with the Father just as He has invited me. Using a walk through the Tabernacle as our paradigm to holiness and godliness, the subsequent chapters of the book will demonstrate the effects each stop inside the Tabernacle has on developing the character of God in a believer, which produces ultimate intimacy in the place of the Holy of Holies. This progression toward godliness will lead one to see the ultimate character of God in a consecrated people. These will be the people, I believe, that point to the Lord Jesus Christ before His soon return in glory.

This book is not for the timid or faint of heart. It is not for the religious who simply want to do their duty on Sunday morning to appease their conscious and God. This book is likewise not for those who purport a belief in the God of the Bible without allowing that belief system to have an impact on their daily lifestyle. This book is for those few serious enough to be drawn into God's secret place because He is ultimately all that really matters. The words of these pages propose a radical call to those who want to give it all back to God by moving in a direction with God that will lead us into the Holy of Holies.

CHAPTER TWO

A BLUEPRINT FROM THE ARCHITECT

One of the all-time and enduring games of children is the game of hide-and-seek. It is a game that in all likelihood you played with childhood friends. It was particularly a great summer's eve pastime outside around the house and in the backyard where there were plenty of trees to hide behind or climb. Whoever was going to hide had to the count of ten to find a secret place. At the count of ten the seeker would say, "Ready or not, here I come."

The pursuit was on. The seeker would proceed to look in every likely spot until successfully saying, "I found you." It seemed that no matter how many times the pursuit was on, there was an expectant excitement in the air. The anticipation of finding your friend was almost as exciting as the actual encounter of finding the friend. The sound of giggles and laughter would then commence together with jumping up and down. An exuberant exchange of, "I thought you were over there behind that bush, but then I heard a sound, so I quickly came over here to find you," could be heard.

The simple game of hide-and-seek reflects the profound pathway to the meaning of life. The human child is called into a game of finding Father God hiding behind the next bush. When the child finds God in the next bush, the same epiphany of life occurs as when you finally located your friend. A manifestation of great presence abounds leaving us in a state of exuberance and joy.

When Moses was led up the mountain at Sinai in pursuit of God, he came across God in a burning bush. God rewarded Moses seeking after Him. He wanted the chase, but He also wanted Moses to find Him. God could not help Himself in the case of Moses that He revealed Himself to Moses in the burning bush. He caught the attention of Moses by the burning bush. The curiosity of Moses peaked. Moses was lured over to God's presence.

The Angel of the Lord appeared to him in flames of fire from within a bush. Moses saw that though the bush was on fire it did not burn up. So Moses thought, "I will go over and see this strange sight—why the bush does not burn up" (Exodus 3:2-3).

A.W. Tozer writes in his classic work *The Pursuit of God*:

We pursue God because, and only because, He has first put an urge within us that spurs us to the pursuit. "No man can come to me," said the Lord, "except the Father which hath sent me draw him," and it is by this prevenient "drawing" that God takes from us every vestige of credit for the act of coming. The impulse to pursue God originates with God, but the outworking of that impulse is our following hard after Him.[i]

The Word of God clearly states that God can be known to all instinctively. *"For since the creation of the world God's invisible qualities—His eternal power and divine nature—have been clearly seen"* (Rom. 1:20). God leaves His signature in creation for us to find. He tells us, *"It is the glory of God to conceal a matter; to search out a matter is the glory of kings"* (Prov. 25:2). Therefore, it is a matter of importance for us who pursue after God to seek revelation. Setting before us the things, which God has concealed, reveals more and more of His glory to us mere mortals.

Like creation, the Word of God itself, the sacred Scriptures reveal hidden knowledge. For example, when one reads the Old Testament in light of the truth that it is written about Jesus Messiah, a new revelation of God's word unfolds. St. Paul understood this truth as he elaborates on the relationship between husband and wife as a relationship between Christ and His Church: *"'For this reason a man will leave his father and mother and be united to his wife, and the two will become one flesh.' This is a profound mystery—but I am talking about Christ and the Church"* (Eph. 5:31-32).

Paul is referring to the revelation that just as Eve was taken out of the side of Adam in the Old Testament, so too the Church is born out of the pierced side of Jesus on Calvary. That which is hidden is now revealed as we pursue after a clearer picture of God.

Jesus Himself often would teach by using parables. He looked to the common things familiar to the people to explain the spiritual nature of the eternal things. For example, He spoke that a mustard seed is like the Kingdom of Heaven, which starts its life out small but eventually grows into a beautiful, large tree. Our life in God starts out small, but grows into something, which pervades and permeates our whole life.

In the Old Testament Scriptures, the Tabernacle of Moses plays a most relevant role. It takes the natural things of creation and transforms them into a language of truth. Not unlike the game of hide-and-seek, God Almighty provides a pathway through which we can find Him.

Tommy Tenney in his book, *The God Chaser*, writes:

God chasers have a lot in common. Primarily, they are not interested in camping out on some dusty truth known to everyone. They are after the fresh presence of the Almighty… If you're a God chaser, you won't be happy to simply follow God's tracks. You will follow them until you apprehend His presence.[ii]

In the game of hide-and-seek, you won't be content finding clues as to where your friend has been or clues as to where your friend might be. You won't be content until you actually stand in their presence. So it is in the pursuit of God. You won't be content with poor substitutes of the real thing. You won't be able to live off an old testimony of what God once did for you. You will need a fresh touch from standing in His presence.

God tells Moses, the leader of the newly formed Jewish people, *"to make this Tabernacle and all its furnishings exactly like the pattern I will show you"* (Exod. 25:8-9). God was instructing them on building of the place where God will meet with man. God promises that in spite of the hardness of hearts in the people, He will continue to dwell in their midst and be their God.

God carefully lays out a plan and pattern for Moses to follow in the building and construction of the Tabernacle. This Tabernacle was to be a place of dwelling for God in the earth, as well as a meeting place for God and man. This dwelling was to be erected in the middle of the camp of the twelve tribes of Israel. It was to have three chambers: an *Outer Court* where the people were allowed to bring there sin offerings, a *Holy Place* where the priests could worship, and a *Most Holy Place* where God resided. Seven pieces of furnishing were instructed by God to be put in the Tabernacle. Two pieces occupied the *Outer Court*, while three pieces occupied the *Holy Place*, with the final two pieces in the *Most Holy Place*. The exact placement of the seven furnishings formed an overhead cross, visible from above only to God Himself.

Each piece offers a progressive, deepening of one's walk with the One, true God. As the priest moved progressively from station to station, he would find that he would be spiritually changed from glory to glory. God chose the pattern of the Tabernacle as an eternal truth about how to deepen our relationship with Him. The foundational truths shown to Moses in the Tabernacle, likewise, show us today how to follow a pattern toward walking in close relationship with God.

The pattern that God revealed in the Tabernacle is as relevant today as it was in Old Testament times. God is not really so interested in our building Him a structure to worship Him. He is interested in us building Him a spiritual life with our lives. *"Don't you know that you yourselves are God's temple, and that God's Spirit lives in you"* (1 Cor. 3:16).

As one walks through the Tabernacle of Moses, one develops an ever increasingly, deeper relationship with our God. The progressive walk through the Tabernacle is a blueprint left by the Architect Himself to guide us in holiness to His presence.

Let me briefly describe for you the overall Tabernacle and then each piece of furnishing within the Tabernacle.

The Tabernacle of Moses

The Books of Exodus and Numbers give detailed descriptions of the Tabernacle; The Book of Leviticus tells us about priestly offerings and sacrifices.. The Book of Hebrews focuses on the concept of the priestly work of Jesus Christ. I will give a brief outline here describing the Tabernacle.

Through the construction of the Tabernacle, God reveals His heart. His deepest desire is to be with us, as He tabernacles among us. The construct of the Tabernacle is decidedly laid out in a manner in which a sinful people can come before a holy God. God is only approachable in holiness, yet He makes a way for man to access His presence.

In Exodus 19 and Numbers 9:1, one finds that the time for constructing the Tabernacle as a portable dwelling took nine months to complete. Like a child being birthed by its mother, like the Word become flesh in Mary, the Tabernacle was built by the word and spirit of God's direction.

The Tabernacle stood in the center of the camp. The 12 tribes of Israel were divided into four groups as they were positioned to surround the structure. On the East the tribes of Judah, Issachar, and Zebulon were positioned under the banner of the lion. On the West the tribes of Ephraim, Mannasseh and Benjamin were positioned under the banner of the ox. On the North the tribes of Dan, Asher, and Naphtali were positioned under the banner of the eagle. While on the South the tribes of Rueben, Simeon, and Gad encamped under the banner of man. The four banners picture the four gospels, which would emanate from the person of Jesus about whom every detail of the structure of the Tabernacle would speak.

A fence of white linen about 7'6" was placed around the Tabernacle area. This linen depicts the righteousness of God, which separates the sacred from the profane. It was hung on silver rods between 60 posts. At the East end stood the only gate to the court. Everyone who wanted to come inside had to enter through the gate. No matter what tribe one was from, the entry to God was the same for all.

The Brazen Altar

Upon entering the *Outer Court* one would be confronted with the Brazen Altar. Sacrificial animals were offered on this Altar. Their blood was shed for the remission of the sin of the people. The word *altar* itself means "lifted up." Its significance is captured in the Gospel of John when Jesus says, *"the son of Man must be **lifted up**, so that everyone who believes in him may have eternal life"* (John 3:14-15).

The Altar was positioned in the Outer Court just inside the gate facing the Tabernacle (see Exod. 40:6). The Altar itself was made of shittim wood. This is an acacia wood, which is indestructible and incorruptible. The son of Man had to be like us in our human nature though He was without sin. The Altar formed a perfect square of five cubits indicating the biblical number for grace. The shittim wood was overlaid with brass, which clearly speaks of judgment on sin in the Old Testament. When God's people sin, judgment is upon them, and heaven is like brass over their heads (see Deuteronomy 28:15-23). There were four horns on the Altar as functional adornments. The animals to be sacrificed were tied to these horns. The fire on the Altar was to burn continually, never to go out. The smell of the stench of burning flesh served as a continual reminder to the Israelites of their sinful nature in need of forgiveness before almighty God.

The Brazen Laver

The Brazen Laver stood beyond the Brazen Altar in the *Outer Court.* The Laver was a reservoir of water used by the priests to wash. God knew the priests would need daily cleansing as they were called to minister to God and to the people. It was a solid brass, round basin which would catch the rainwater from the night before. It is interesting to note that the large round basin would create a reflection during the daylight hours, acting like a magnifying glass to each priest who would approach it for cleansing. Each priest would see himself for what he was, and consequently be reminded of his need for cleansing from his sinful human nature. The exterior of the Laver was brass, which speaks of this sinful nature.

The Golden Lampstand

Leaving the Brazen Laver, the priest would approach the Tabernacle properly and enter into the Holy Place to meet with God. There were three pieces of furniture in the Holy Place. The solid-gold Lampstand stood to the south side, or the left side, of the room. This was a candlestick with seven branches, with a large center shaft extending higher than the other six branches on either side of the center shaft. It spoke of the glory of God lighting up the people of Israel. The Lampstand used oil lamps, not candles. It continually burned by a supply of oil poured into the lamps. The beautiful Lampstand illuminated all that was in the Holy Place. It was meant as a demonstration of the light of God to priests who followed Him. The hammers of the goldsmith beat the golden candlestick. What emerged was a thing of beauty. Pure olive oil was used for the light.

The Table of Showbread

The Table of Showbread stood opposite the Lampstand on the north side, or right side, of the Tabernacle in the Holy Place. The table was made of shittim wood, and it was overlaid in gold. It was two cubits in length, one and one-half cubits high, and one cubit wide. A gold rim encircled the table's top. The table had gold rings. Acacia wood covered in gold went through the rings to carry the table.

On the table, 12 loaves of bread represented the 12 tribes of Israel. The 12 loaves were arranged in rows of six each. The bread was unleavened because it was to be an offering. The term *showbread* means "bread of the face" or "bread of presence."

The fragrance of the freshly baked bread with frankincense sprinkled over it filled the Holy Place. There were serving vessels made into bread pans with spoons for incense poured over the bread to be burned on the Altar of Incense.

The Golden Altar of Incense

The Golden Altar of Incense was positioned in the Holy Place before the veil. The Altar was for the burning of the incense before the Lord. The incense always speaks of the prayers and intercessions of the saints being lifted up before God. The Golden Altar was much smaller than the Brazen Altar, but it is the highest piece of furniture in the Tabernacle. This speaks to the highest honor God puts on the ministry of intercession. It was made of acacia wood, and it was covered in gold with gold rings and horns at each square corner.

Incense consisted of three perfumes mixed with frankincense. Stacte, onycha, and galbanum were mixed to form half the composition, while pure frankincense formed the other half. These gums and spices are extracted from trees or the sea then beaten and blended into fine powder. God instructed Moses that the incense be most pure and sweet to His senses. Aaron, the high priest, offered incense every morning while the rest of the priests offered ministry unto God throughout the day and night. These offerings were not a burnt offering, or a meal offering, or a drink offering. The call by God for *"fire on the altar"* (Exod. 30:20) is a clear call for intercessory prayer.

The Structure of the Tabernacle

The structure of the Tabernacle itself consisted of 48 planks of wood overlaid in gold, which were set in 96 silver sockets. The implication here is that God's glory (gold) needs to rest upon the work of His redemptive Son (silver). These planks stood in their sockets and were braced by five planks on each of the three sides, which were closed. The doorway had a linen hanging and was held up by five pillars.

Holy of Holies

At the opposite end of the Holy Place was found another hanging called the "veil" which covered the entrance to the Holy of Holies. Curtains and coverings were draped over the structure acting as a roof for the Tabernacle.

The multi-colored veil was embroidered with the likeness of cherubim. The veil acted as a separation or barrier between God and man. The curtain hung from gold hooks supported by four pillars of acacia wood overlaid with golden anchors in four sockets of silver. The veil didn't totally shut out man from God's presence. Once a year, the high priest could enter the Holy of Holies on the Day of Atonement to offer blood on the Mercy Seat for sin.

He entered three times on the Day of Atonement. First, he entered with a censor of hot coals. The Shekinah cloud of God's glory filled the room. Next, the high priest took the blood of a freshly slain bullock and entered again to sprinkle the Mercy Seat over the Ark of the Covenant with its blood. Finally, the high priest took an offering of a slain male goat's blood in the Holy of Holies

The layout of the Holy Place was 20 cubits (30 ft.) in length and 10 cubits (15 ft.) wide. The Holy of Holies with the Ark of the Covenant was 10 cubits square (15 sq. ft.). The veil separating the two rooms was woven from three colors: blue (the color of Heaven), scarlet (the color of blood), and purple (the color of royalty). Every detail of its construction had revelatory significance, and every detail was given to Moses by the command of the Lord Most High.

The Ark of the Covenant

If we were permitted to gaze beyond the curtain, we would be privileged to see the Ark of the Covenant. It served as a majestic display of God's presence; by far the most sacred furnishing in the Tabernacle. The Ark was a chest of acacia wood, overlaid with pure gold inside and outside. It measured two and one-half cubits long, by one and one-half cubits wide, by one and one-half cubits high. Hebrews 9:4 describes the three objects contained in the Ark: the golden pot of manna, the rod of Aaron that budded, and the tablets of the Law.

The golden pot that had manna was the food provided by God for the Israelites during their sojourn in the desert for 40 years. The manna appeared each morning around the camp of the Israelites when the dew fell on the ground like a hoary frost. Aaron was directed by God to collect manna in a golden bowl and place it in the Ark. The manna reveals God's provision to meet our every need.

Aaron's budded rod was placed in the Ark as a sign of authority. It is recorded in the Book of Numbers that Aaron and Moses were challenged by other men regarding their rightful authority to lead the people. God directed Moses to collect an almond rod from each of the 12 tribes with the name of the tribe engraved on it. This was done to determine who had the right to be high priest. All the rods were placed in the Tabernacle overnight. The rod of the priest God had chosen as high priest would blossom and yield almonds. The next morning Aaron's rod was the one that budded. This clearly demonstrated he alone had the right to be high priest. It needs to be noted that the rod not only budded, but it also bore fruit. (see Num. 17:1-11).

Tablets of the Law were engraved in stone. Although the first set of Tablets was broken, a second set was placed in the Ark. (see Deut. 10:1-2). Even before Moses could give the Law of the Commandments to the nation of Israel, Israel's sinful idolatry was realized in their worship of the golden calf. (see Exod. 32:1). This made evident the truth that man cannot keep the Law on his own willpower, and that the purpose of the Law was to make evident man's sinful nature. It is not surprising, then, that the Tablets of the Law were placed in the Ark under the Mercy Seat.

The Mercy Seat

The Mercy Seat was the lid for the Ark of the Covenant. It was made of one piece of gold with two cherubim at each end of the Mercy Seat facing each other.

The wingspan of the two cherubim extended one toward the other with the blood stained Mercy Seat between them. The significance of the one-in-three Godhead can be witnessed here.

The Book of Hebrews uses the Greek word "propitiation" for Mercy Seat. It is the blood that has become our propitiation, or Mercy Seat. If one were to take away the lid of the Mercy Seat, one would be exposed to the operation of the Law. This would mean death to all since the wages of sin is death for all (see Rom. 6:23). It is likewise significant to remember that this piece of furniture is called a *seat*, meaning that judgment is removed from all that apply the blood sacrifice from the One who is seated on this throne.

Now that I have summarized the structure of the Tabernacle of Moses with each of its furnishings, let me now turn to a theological understanding of the relevancy of the Tabernacle of Moses to the people of Israel.

Israel, unlike her neighboring peoples and tribes, was a monotheistic, religious people. Their religious tenets came forth from revelation that God was one. For Judaism, Deuteronomy 6:4 has come to be known as their confession of faith. *"Hear O Israel: The Lord our God, the Lord is One."*

Even to this modern day, Jews around the world recite this passage daily as a matter of prayerful faith in God's sovereign Lordship over their lives. Likewise, they believed as a people in offering atonement for their sins through the offering of blood in animal sacrifices.

The Book of Leviticus presents an overwhelming message on the importance of the people of Israel to be holy so that they might come to God Most Holy. As a matter of fact, the key passage to the Book of Leviticus is found in the words, *"You must be holy because I, the Lord your God, am holy"* (Lev. 19:2). Therefore, there had to be a way available to the people to deal with their sinfulness. This is why we read in the Book of Leviticus about the institution of the Levitical priesthood to make sacrifices for the sins of the people.

Sin could be purged from the people, so that the people could come before the holiness of God. The detailed instructions and procedures for sacrifice outlined in the opening chapters of the Book of Leviticus offer the people of Israel a way to God. Whether the sacrifice is a goat, bull, sheep, or a turtledove, it must be without blemish or defect. The priest offered the sacrifice to the one true God in behalf of the Israelite's sin, so that payment was made to God for the offense against Him and His Law.

CHAPTER THREE

OUTSIDE THE GATE (THE TABERNACLE AT A DISTANCE)

One day Peter and John were going up to the temple at the time of prayer- at three in the afternoon. Now a man crippled from birth was being carried to the temple gate called Beautiful, where he was put every day to beg from those going into the temple courts. When he saw Peter and John about to enter, he asked them for money. Peter looked straight at him, as did John. Then Peter said, "Look at us!" So the man gave them his attention, expecting to get something from them. Then Peter said, "Silver or gold I do not have, but what I have I give you. In the name of Jesus Christ of Nazareth, walk. Taking him by the right hand, he helped him up, and instantly the man's feet and ankles became strong. He jumped to his feet and began to walk. He then went with them into the temple courts, walking and jumping, and praising God. When all the people saw him walking and praising God, they recognized him as the same man who used to sit begging at the temple gate called Beautiful, and they were filled with wonder and amazement at what had happened to him (Acts 3:1-10).

This narrative account takes place in New Testament times during the early stages of the followers of Jesus. The Temple that Jesus preached in before his death is the same Temple that Peter and John were entering for prayer. The Temple of Jerusalem, like its predecessor, Solomon's Temple, was patterned after the same basic directives, which God gave to Moses for the building of the Tabernacle. As we recall, the Tabernacle was surrounded by a courtyard that is surrounded by a fence of linen with a gate of entrance.

The crippled man represents all those who have not entered in through the gate. Many, many in the world are sitting like the beggar outside the gate waiting for someone to come along to bring him into the Temple. Yet, millions sit in a crippled condition outside the courts of God. Entering into the courts of our God through the gate is the beginning of one's journey into God's presence. Like the beggar we must come empty handed to God. The beggar did come empty handed, but day after day he settled for less than what God could give him. He sat outside the courts of God, as he was accustomed for years begging for alms, when God had His glory to offer him.

It may even be said that in some places in the Church, some have lost sight of the glory of God's greatness, and have found themselves sitting like the crippled begging for a few measly morsels of bread to get by for the day. They have unfortunately accommodated themselves to a false imitation of God rather than the reality of God. They may even have *"a form of godliness but lack the power therein"* (2 Tim. 3:5). Peter was an eyewitness to God's glory. He entered into the presence of the Lord. He desired not so much to know about God, but to know God. He desired more from God.

Peter witnessed Jesus healing the sick, forgiving the sinner, and raising the dead. He was baptized in the fire of God. When he came upon the cripple beggar, he did not hand him money. He said that he had no silver or gold, but he gave what he had. What he had was burning alive inside him. As a church, many have made a way of life handing out morsels. This is a poor substitute for the glory of the Lord. Many have lost sight of their true inheritance in God. God is calling all the while for us to come to Him for our full inheritance. Many have come to expect little from God. With little expectation comes little in return. By forfeiting our expectancy, many forfeit the full loaf of fresh bread for a few crumbs and morsels. By reducing their expectancy, many reduce what God can deliver into their hands.

The instant Peter and John come along the path of the crippled beggar, they shatter an institution of thinking that had become sacrosanct. Like iconoclasts they break with the thinking of the day that God couldn't or wouldn't heal the cripple. Taking the man by the right hand, he is strengthened by word, power, and example. Just as the expectations of the crippled man are raised, so too is he raised out of his former state of mind and body.

Hungry for the Real Thing

The only way in which it is acceptable for us to be beggars is if we come before God empty handed and hungry. The Syrophoenician woman in the Gospel begged Jesus to drive out the demon from her daughter. He says, *"First let the children* (the Jews) *eat all they want, for it is not right to take the children's bread and toss it to their dogs."* She replied, *"But even the dogs eat the crumbs from the children"* (Mark 7:25-30). Because of her refusal to give up or give in, the Lord rewarded her. Our hunger for God and our persistence for the inheritance of God always gets God's attention. The word of God teaches that the *"violent take the kingdom of God by force"* (Matt. 11:12). We need to leave our manners behind as we press in for more. Somehow we have permitted the secular world to influence our beliefs more than the truth of God's word. God rewards those who diligently seek Him. Desperation, neediness, and violent intercession win over God's heart. Desperation, neediness, and violent intercession cause the breakthrough to come.

Out of the Darkness

Acts 3:17, 19 says, *"Brothers, I know that you acted out of ignorance as did your leaders...Repent, turn to God, so that your sins may be wiped out; that times of refreshing such as what you've seen may come."* The word of God teaches, *"My people are destroyed from lack of knowledge"* (Hos. 4:6). The Greek word for "ignorance" is also the same word for "darkness." To live in ignorance of the truth is to live in darkness. God calls us to live in the light. We need to repent of our darkened minds, and live in the light of the truth. Then, times of refreshing will come as we are led into the presence of our God.

We clearly know that those outside the gate do not have knowledge of the God of revelation. Some religions teach that there are many paths to God. They teach that each religion has its own kernel of truth. However, the God of the Bible unequivocally states that Jesus in the flesh is the visible reality of the invisible God. Jesus is the Gate. A revelation of God comes from entering into a personal relationship with Jesus. We meet Him by an act of faith at the gate. This invitation to enter in is extended to all. The acceptance of the invitation must be a personal, heartfelt response to Jesus as Savior. Therefore, we cannot come into this relationship by mere virtue of being born into a Christian denomination. Religion doesn't save; only Jesus does.

Nominal Christians, who in a sense are born into a family religion, have not yet come into personal relationship with Jesus. Individuals who have accepted the religious tenets of the Christian religion have not necessarily made a transition to a personal relationship with Jesus. Going to church and following Law and moral code is not what this is all about. Fulfilling obligations and even performing works of charity and philanthropy do not cause one to enter into the Kingdom of God. Grace is not cheap. It came at the price of the Savior's death. It would be presumptuous to believe that one could buy one's way to God by works. A friend of mine once told me of his friend dying in a hospital. The man who was an unbeliever said he had lived a clear life and had tried to do good during the course of his life. He then said, "Why would I not go to heaven?" My friend Ray replied, "You have never accepted or honored God's Son."

Yet, there are many avid seekers of the truth today. They are well aware of their spiritual compass and are seeking after spiritual fulfillment. They want a close encounter with God of a supernatural kind. They want to taste and see how good the Lord is. One moment with Him will change every moment thereafter. One moment touched by Jesus will make every other moment outside the gate pale into insignificance. At one moment God was a remote, idealistic thought; the next moment He becomes real in our lives. One moment God is possibly just a supreme being; the next moment He becomes our most intimate friend.

God's word clearly teaches that His presence dwells in His creation. We need only to read Psalm 139 to comprehend this truth. In essence, the verses spell out God's presence as something hidden yet something revealed in creation. The author of creation left not only His fingerprints in His handiwork, but He also abides in His creation! This is an awesome thought. God lives in His creation, yet He is not limited by it. He is so much greater than the sum of its parts.

What I am trying to articulate is the doctrine of the transcendence of God as well as the immanence of God. The doctrine of divine presence does not assume pantheism. Things that are ultimately corruptible and transient cannot define God's glory. He is above all His works while simultaneously immanent with them. This is precisely why we can say God is everywhere. Whether or not we are aware of this truth, it does not alter the truth. God is ever-present in space and time. It is the encounter with God that opens the door to the world of His presence. Our born-again close encounter leaves us with new senses. These new senses perceive God and life in a revolutionary way. Our relationship with Him becomes the most exciting relationship ever had.

CHAPTER FOUR

THE ESSENTIAL DECISION (THE BRAZEN ALTAR)

The Brazen Altar had but one purpose. It stood as a burning ground for the sins of the people of Israel. The guilt from sins had to be atoned. Prescribed animal offerings were brought at any time of day or night to the gate of the Tabernacle. The priest who received the live offering at the gate had the Israelite touch the unblemished animal's head.

By laying their hand on the head of the innocent lamb, the Israelite was transferring the guilt of sin upon the lamb. The substitution of the lamb for the Israelite freed the Israelite from the judgment of God upon sin. Justification came through faith in the blood sacrifice. The priest then took the animal to the Brazen Altar to be killed. A basin caught the dripping blood from the animal's throat that had been cut. The priest sprinkled the blood from the basin on the horns of the Altar of Sacrifice, cut the animals body into pieces, washed the internal organs clean, and burned the pieces on the Altar as a sweet-smelling savor.

The Altar is positioned in the Outer Court facing the Tabernacle entrance. No priest could approach the Tabernacle proper without offering sacrifice. To approach God without a sin offering meant certain death. This is the place of God where judgment is changed to mercy. One is declared righteous or in right relationship with God. No son of Adam can come to God without an acceptable substitute offered for sin.

Original Sin

Since the fall of Adam, original sin touches and contaminates every single human being. No one can escape it. Heredity, genetics, biology, and even the environment are tainted with and by original sin. No child enters this world as a "blank slate." The prevalent and widespread notion that learning theory is totally responsible for the development of the personality is false and deceptive. One enters this world with a predisposition to certain disease and sickness, as well as psychological traits stemming from an inborn propensity toward selfishness. As beautiful as a newborn baby appears, it is nonetheless already tainted by original sin.

Sin does not seem to be a very popular subject for discussion. Yet, it was something that the Israelites were reminded of every day for nearly 500 years as the Brazen Altar burned with violent, bloody death. We on the other hand, in order to sooth our consciences, have gone to great lengths to embrace the philosophy of situation ethics, which helps us to deny any wrongdoing. We mistakably believe that, "if it feels right, then do it as long as it doesn't hurt anybody else." Ours is an age of tolerance and political correctness. Tolerance of others is a religious dictum. If one forms a judgment or an opinion excluding anyone or taking exception to the popular agenda, then one is labeled as intolerant.

This approach to morality has made the majority of our society anesthetized to sin. Most of us need a shaking to awaken us to our sinful human nature. The purpose of this shaking would not be to heap coals of guilt, but to drive us to God's mercy. One might say that we have slowly, methodically, and deliberately been lulled to sleep. We have become seasoned sinners without an awareness of our sin. Our eyes, for example, are bombarded with stimulus and imagery that is violent and abusive. What was once thought as unthinkable has gained its way into the mainstream as acceptable and permissive. We have made idols of things. We have seen our decisions coerced, compromised by the things of the world. We are tainted by sin and don't really recognize it. Most believers don't seem to be too much different than non-believers.

Ever since Cain killed his brother Abel the battle of sin has raged. The heart is deceitful above all things (see Jer. 17:9). We must be sensitized to sin again if ever we are to progress in the path of holiness. The Brazen Altar stood as a monolith in the midst of the people as a reminder of the need to come before God as a sinner. The word of God warns about being lukewarm, *"I know that you are neither hot nor cold. I wish that you were either one or the other"* (Rev. 3:15).

We need to be aware and watchful over our lives. It is ever so easy to be coerced. The Bible tells us to test the spirits (see 1 John 4:1-6). We need to discern whether a thing is from God. The word says, *"Enter through the narrow gate. For wide is the gate and broad is the road that leads to destruction, and many enter through it. But small is the gate and narrow the road that leads to life, and only a few find it"* (Matt. 7:13-14).

Salvation

For me this realization came as I found myself in a place of need. I had an office of priest that placed me in a unique position. But the position had its constraints. It demanded that I know Him whom I preached. Something was wrong with my relationship with God. I spoke about Him. I taught about Him, but I did not know Him personally. There had to be some way to really come to know God. I had to find out.

At the same time I found myself seeking after the reality of God, I was quickly burning out from all my obligations as a pastor in a large church. At age 25, I labored under an ethic of works and performance. Just to prepare a Sunday sermon was such a burden. I delighted if a visiting missionary came through on a Sunday just so I didn't have to preach. God's word did console me when He said, *"Come to Me, all you who are weary and burdened, and I will give you rest...for My yoke is easy and My burden is light"* (Matt. 11:28,30). Could it be that my burden was heavy because I needed to come to Him? Could it be that I really didn't know Him personally?

I bent down on my knees in my bedroom. I quietly sobbed. I cried out for God to do something in me. At this point I knew He was in the room with me. His presence and peace started to come over me even as I continued to weep. He gave me a reassurance that He saved me from my own demise. No longer would I have to prove myself as a person or priest. I no longer had to live up to an image of "a good priest." I knew before I wasn't so good; now I knew only He was good. In spite of not being good, I was still acceptable to Him. I spent a lifetime striving, achieving, and performing. In an instant, it was gone. Something broke inside. If God loved me and accepted me, then it really didn't matter if others accepted me. In my weakness and limitations I learned the lesson of self-acceptance. In accepting myself, I accepted His grace and holiness working in me.

This testimony relates to the Brazen Altar because anything that our flesh produces is attributable to our pride. What God accomplishes through us is attributable to Him working in us. The new perspective on life turned things upside down. I no longer had to hold myself out to the public as holy and good anymore. I could now simply be a sinner like everyone else who was changed through His mercy and grace. Living under the weight of performance was gone. Living under the weight of condemnation and guilt was gone. Like Peter, I concentrated on Jesus and hung up my sin. Unlike Judas, I no longer concentrated on sin thereby hanging myself. I knew of the precious gift of God's love.

I believe the Lord is calling us into His holiness and righteousness. Trespasses in our lives must be cut out and left with God forever. We are called to separate ourselves from sin. For God is preparing a Bride for His son to be without stain or wrinkle. The purifying fire of judgment is at work dividing and separating flesh and spirit, light and darkness, righteousness and sin. The fire is clarifying the difference between the Kingdom of God and the kingdom of evil. The pillar of fire is to purge and purify. The transformation can produce a further revelation of the sons and daughters of God.

Recently, I heard in my spirit these words:

I am calling forth a remnant to be my Bride. I must separate anything that holds you back or binds you to sin. Expect change in your life. Relationships will change; attitudes will change. What you once thought of as important you no longer revere. What you once depended on, you no longer depend upon. Things you formerly loved are now disdained. The fire is never pleasant. But remember, in the midst of the fire I am present. My purpose in the fire is to separate and sanctify until it is glorified. It isn't until you are separated and sanctified that you are glorified. I am bringing forth sons of thunder, daughters of light, children of My glory. I want you to mature, and be perfected in My Holiness. I will have My way before I return.

The Book of Joshua teaches that hidden sin cuts God's provision short. Unconfessed sin cuts God's provision short because God Himself will not mix with sin. This principle is taught in the story of Joshua and one of his generals, Achan. In Joshua 7:12b, God says, *"I will not be with you anymore unless you destroy whatever among you is devoted to destruction."* The devoted things were the spoils of war taken from the vanquished people of Jericho, which God deemed, in this case, idolatrous. God had given Joshua specific instructions for his troops not to take any devoted things from Jericho for themselves. These things were considered unholy and idolatrous before God. Achan coveted a beautiful imported robe, some gold, and money taken in the victory over Jericho.

At times God allowed for the booty of victory to be taken by His conquering army. However, on this occasion directives were given to refrain. God knew of Achan's actions and informed Joshua that there was sin in the camp. He was told his army would no be able to stand against even the weakest of enemies until the sin was removed from the camp.

Achan and his family were exposed and stoned to death for their disobedience to Joshua's commands not to take the devoted things unto themselves. We may not be stoned to death; nevertheless, the wages of sin is still death. God's provision will be cut off from our lives until we deal with our sin. Our foundational life needs to be built upon God's holiness and His righteousness. The foundation can be built on no man, but on God.

God will not grace us and bless us if we refuse to deal with the sin in our life. Things like cursing, criticism, cutting remarks, raging, abusive behavior, anger, violence, assault, and harshness are but a few of the common sins in the lives of people. Rebellion, narcissism, lying, cheating, stealing, and murder are others. These and other sins bring destruction upon us. We have got to be cleaned up. The way has been paved for us to be made clean. The atonement is accomplished. God has made a way.

In the Book of Judges one finds the story of Samson. Here, this strongest of men from the tribe of Dan, desires and lusts after a young, Philistine woman. Samson's parents caution him that she is a pagan and not an Israelite. Samson pays no heed to his parents, and promises to marry her. On his way to Timnah where he first laid eyes on her, Samson encounters a lion. He rips apart the lion barehanded and leaves its dead carcass off the path. The Bible says, *"He later turned off the path to look at the carcass of the lion. He found that a swarm of bees had made some honey in the carcass. He scooped out some of the honey into his hands and ate it along the way"* (Judges 14:8-9).

Because sin has the appearance of honey, it entices us with its apparent sweetness. Samson held on to the sweetness of the honey that resulted in death. God's word tells us to touch nothing unclean. The anointing of Samson diminished after this point in his life. He may have lost his gift of strength when Delilah cut his hair, but his own arrogance caused his downfall, for he disobeyed the laws of his

God. Hanging on to "dead" things in our lives will only serve to cut us off from God's presence. Let go of pornography, adultery, fornication, deceit, and all occult practices.

It has been said that the Outer Court is the place of justification before God. The judicial act of God in the likeness of the Brazen Altar was made complete in the sacrifice of Jesus Christ as the Lamb of God who takes away the sin of the whole world. The Altar of Sacrifice of the Old Covenant foreshadowed the New Covenant Altar that is the sacrifice of Jesus on the cross.

Justification was bought at the price of our Savior's death. It does not depend on any work from us. Jesus, the perfect Lamb, unblemished and pure, freely gave up His life for our sins. *"He was delivered over to death for our sins, and was raised to life for our justification"* (Rom. 4:25). The blood of Jesus spilt on Calvary proves that His death has taken place for our death in sin. His death gives the power of new life to any that would accept its power. To receive the miracle of life requires that one only submit to Jesus as Savior. This is the most important step toward God. It is the step that takes one into the Kingdom of Heaven.

Revelation 1:15 states in John's words that Jesus appeared to him, *"with feet like bronze glowing in the furnace."* Here one has a clear reference to Jesus as the Brazen Altar. It is interesting to note that the word *altar* means "high places." In this context it indicates that Jesus was sacrificed to bring down the high places of hell. That is why Jesus can confidently say, *"If I be lifted up from the earth, I will draw all men to Me*" (John 12:32). His sacrifice is an eternal fire burning on the Altar heralding God's love for humankind.

The sacrifice of Jesus on the cross, then, speaks of the believer's justification. One is now declared righteous by the death of Jesus Christ, and therefore lives in right relationship before God. The Bible says that without the shedding of blood there can be no forgiveness of sin. Our precious Lord Jesus suffered and died in the place of humankind, that all might be forgiven their sins.

The paradox of the redeeming cross, efficacious for the salvation of the whole world, stares blatantly at that world it so desperately wants to embrace. In an act of humiliation and pain, the divine heart of God willed freely to give His sinless life for sinners. In Christ, the world was reconciled to Himself (see 2 Cor. 5:19); after sin had made us His enemies (see Rom. 5:10).

Power Over the Enemy

The Outer Court is the place where sin is forgiven, but it may also be described as a place of spiritual warfare. One should remember that as Jesus died on the cross of Calvary, He descended into hell signifying His victory over sin, death, and evil. Revelation 1:17-18 says, "*Do not be afraid; I am the first and the last, and the living One; and I was dead, and behold, I am alive forevermore, and I hold the keys of death and Hades.*" The public ministry of Jesus was critically tied to two elements: (1) the proclamation of the good news that the Kingdom of God had come and (2) the demonstration of its power through the casting out of demons. The ministry of Jesus cannot be understood without dealing with the devil and demons. The sacred Scriptures back the reality of evil. Unfortunately for some, the rate at which demon possession is diagnosed is inversely proportional to their education in the behavioral sciences.

The devil understands the power of the blood. The word of God teaches us, *"the law requires that nearly everything be cleansed with blood, and without the shedding of blood there is no forgiveness"* (Heb. 9:22). The very time that Jesus died, the Jews were in prayer because it was the Passover. The Jews remembered the time when God said, *"When I see the blood I will pass over you"* (Exodus 12:23). To all who believe in the sacrifice of Jesus and the efficacy of His blood, there is freedom and protection from sin and the curse of the enemy.

The blood speaks of atonement as the high priest took the blood of goats and bulls and went beyond the veil of the Holy Place once a year to sprinkle the Mercy Seat in the name of the people (see Heb. 9:27). If he had not offered blood, he would have been stricken down. To plead the blood of Jesus is to confess our total dependency on His mercy. Hebrews 9:12 says, *"But he entered the Most Holy Place once for all by his own blood, having obtained eternal redemption."* This means that through His death and shedding of blood, Jesus the High Priest sprinkled His blood on the throne of God in Heaven.

The blood of Jesus is a most powerful tool in prayer against the evil one. We read in the word of God of a great conflict in the last days between satan and man.

Then I heard a loud voice in heaven say: "Now have come the salvation and the power and the kingdom of our God, and the authority of his Christ. For the accuser of our brothers, who accuses them before our God day and night, has been hurled down. They overcame him by the blood of the Lamb and by the word of their testimony (Revelation 12:10-11).

We overcome evil when we testify personally to what the word of God says, namely what the blood of Jesus does. The blood of Jesus redeems us from the grasp of the enemy. The Son of God came to destroy the works of the devil. As the old, familiar hymn says, "There is power, power, mighty, saving power in the precious blood of the Lamb."

November 2000, I went on a spiritual pilgrimage to Argentina. I went to visit a crusade gathering held by Carlos Annacondia. Revival is sweeping across that land in great waves of power since the 1980s. It has been reported that a city of 1 million might have 400,000 saved during the course of his crusades. Annacondia has shaken the nation of Argentina through the power of his crusades. I watched closely and listened attentively to everything this man did. I was struck by his unique blend of compassion and authority—a blend that was present in Jesus Himself. Annacondia spoke right to where the people were living. This meeting was not about piety. It was a practical message, which offered deliverance and freedom from the chains of addiction.

Literally, hundreds of people stepped forward for the invitation to accept Christ as Savior. However, before he prayed for salvation, he called out the demons of hell that had many of the people in bondage to drugs, alcohol, lust, infirmity, cancer, depression, and so on. People began to shriek and fall to the ground. Assistants at the crusade picked up people from the ground and led them into the tent of deliverance. Carlos has said there is a major difference between Argentina's prayer ministries and those in the United States. In Argentina the people are set free. In the United States the people get saved, but they are not generally liberated from their bondage.

People bound by an addiction may accept Christ in an American crusade. They rejoice because God has forgiven their sins, yet they find themselves still addicted to the very thing that brought them to Christ in the first place. They are stuck in the addiction and often feel guiltier than when they first went to the crusade. It is not enough that an individual is forgiven. The individual needs to be set free. The Church must journey farther into the realm of setting the captives free. The liberation of the saints, in fact the liberation of all, is essential that humankind see a demonstration of the power of God.

In 1997, a group of intercessors for New England gathered in Salem, Massachusetts on Halloween. They gathered to pray for the blood that was shed during the Salem witch trials. They prayed with a spirit of repentance for the sins of men against these women, to ask God for forgiveness for the historical occurrences that took place on Gallows Hill, and to reclaim the town for the Lord. They broke bread with some of the descendents of the victims who were hanged. This reconciliation service hopefully helped to lay an ax to the occult roots in Salem and brought some healing to the land. When innocent blood is shed, great power comes forth out of the shedding of blood. In the case of Salem, the blood of their martyrs spurred on the cause of witchcraft.

Power over the enemy illustrates that two kingdoms are opposed one to another. The Kingdom of God is in opposition to the kingdom of the darkness. The sacrifice of Jesus' death demonstrates the ultimate victory of the kingdom of God over the kingdom of darkness. Every believer must take this truth and apply it to their circumstances for victory. For believers to overcome, they must recognize this truth and practically apply it just as the Israelites applied the blood to the door on the first Passover in Egypt. Demons are extremely legalistic. They know their rights, and they know when their rights are stripped from them. Casting out demons should be a common, ordinary work of a believer.

It is true this belief can be taken to an extreme; we are not advocating extremism here. However, our church life in general has abdicated its role of deliverance ministry.

It needs to be restored to its proper place. Evangelism will again assume its full effectiveness as ministry again recognizes demonic oppression and the power of deliverance. As expelling demons was a normal part of Jesus' ministry, delivering the oppressed should become a normal part of the ministry of evangelism.

It is interesting to note that blood in the natural is the carrier of life to the body. The substance of blood carries life. The American Red Cross has long been known in its fine work of creating blood banks for life support. It should not be surprising to us that life is in the blood for the believer. That special blood which flowed out from the person of Jesus continues to offer spiritual nourishment and eternal life today.

Maxwell Whyte described it this way in his classic edition of *The Power of the Blood* (Whitaker House, 1973) when he writes, "Peter rightly describes it (Jesus' blood) as *precious blood*" (1 Pet. 1:19). It is not possible to evaluate the blood of Jesus by human values. It is priceless. It is God's price for the redemption of the whole human race.

God provides the most effectual blood of all prefigured in the Outer Court of the Tabernacle of Moses. It is a provision for the forgiveness of our sin and our deliverance from evil.

Derek Prince writes of these provisions in his book *Atonement* (Chosen Books, 2000). Prince says:

> *On the cross, as we have seen, a divinely ordained exchange took place—something conceived in the heart and mind of God from eternity and acted out at Calvary. The cross was no accident—not some grievous mishap forced on Jesus, or some development God had not foreseen. No, the cross was a marvel ordained by God from the beginning of time in which Jesus, as Priest, offered Himself to God as the sacrifice. By this one sacrifice He made provision for all the needs of the whole human race in every area of our lives, for time and for eternity.*[iii]

Prince then makes this remarkable statement:

> *The nature of this exchange was this: All the evil due by justice to us came on Jesus, that all the good due to Jesus, because of His sinless obedience, might be made available to us. Or, more briefly: All the evil came on Jesus that all the good might be made available to us.?*

In essence, the Outer Court's stench of death in the shedding of the blood speaks of the divine exchange of His death for our life.

CHAPTER FIVE

RENEWED (BRAZEN LAVER)

The Greek myth of Narcissus is the story of the teenage youth that looks at his reflection in the water and falls in love with himself. Gazing upon his image, he falls head over heels into the water and drowns. As a psychological formation, *narcissism* serves as a metaphoric term for a type of self-absorption that quite likely resulted from a culture that put such high priority on status, image, and accomplishment.

Narcissism has worked its way into the DSM-IV category of Personality Disorders. This is the professional psychiatric manual for diagnosing mental disorders. *Narcissism* is defined as "a pervasive pattern of grandiosity beginning in early adulthood and present in various contexts. It is indicated by a hyper-reaction to criticism, an interpersonal exploitation, exaggerated sense of self-importance, fantasies of unlimited brilliance, beauty or success, a unique sense of entitlement, and a stunning lack of empathy and compassion for others."[iv]

Psychoanalyst Otto Kernberg writes in *Borderline Conditions and Pathological Narcissism* (Jason Aronson, 1975) that narcissism develops as a necessary precondition to object love.

"As the boundaries between the self and the world around begin to become more defined, an important differentiation takes hold. Namely, that the child is in this world separate from and other than its mother and the world. Up until this point, the child saw its suckling mother as a simple appendage to be used to satisfy its need for gratification. The mother is perceived as having no existence on her own.

The recognition by the child that it is not the center of the universe presents a rude wakeup call to the child. However, most children learn to adapt to this reality of life and continue to develop normally. At times, the young child can feel so unloved and not affirmed that it begins to "bend itself" toward the creature, gaining its identity there rather than from its Creator."[v]

C. S. Lewis writes in *The Four Loves* (Harcourt, Brace and Co., 1960) of a more common developmental problem than the mythological tale of self-indulgence. He says:

We are born helpless. As soon as we are fully conscious we discover loneliness. Born lonely, we try hard to fit in, to be the kind of person that will cause others to like us. Craving and needing very much the affirmation of others, we compromise, put on any face, or many faces; we do even those things we do not like to do in order to fit in.[vi]

In any circumstance, it is difficult growing up. We all come into this world flawed and in need, and we all grow up in this world with flaws and in need. Even though we one day discover the beauty of love in God and receive God into our hearts, there still remains in us all the unwanted character flaws and needs.

God in His goodness has again made provision for our character flaws and needs. These provisions are made at the Laver of water. The blood speaks of the cross, and water speaks of the word of God. The blood addresses our position before God, and the water addresses our state or condition before God. Although one is found righteous before God through the blood of Jesus, one is still defiled and contaminated in their human personality. This is why God in His gracious supply gives us the Laver at which we can wash.

As the priest would wash in the Laver, his reflection would come back at him through the mirror of the water. He would be forced to inspect himself to see if he be counted worthy to go on into the Holy Place. The Book of Psalms says:

Who may climb the mountain of the Lord? Who may stand in His holy place? Only those whose hands and hearts are pure, who do not worship idols and never tell lies. They will receive the Lord's blessing and have right standing with God their Savior. They alone may enter God's presence and worship the God of Israel (Psalm 24:3-6 NLV).

The Laver then is the place for the sanctification of the heart. Some believers are under the mistaken notion that once they are saved that every sin disappears from their life. Paul says, *"...offer yourselves to God, as those who have been brought from death to life; and offer the parts of your body to Him as instruments of righteousness"* (Rom. 6:13). The members of our body still need to come under the washing in the word. It is God's word that brings about the necessary changes within. One must grow up in Him in all things (see Eph. 4:15).

The Laver reveals the filth residing in the flesh. It cleanses and refreshes thus preparing the Spirit to enter the Holy Place. The Holy Spirit needs to overcome one's sinful passions and evil desires. He calls one to put to death every selfish and sinful desire. The word says, *"Since, then, you have been raised with Christ, set your hearts on things above, where Christ is seated at the right hand of God. Set your minds on things above, not on earthly things. For you died, and your life is now hidden with Christ in God"* (Col. 3:1-3).

Adam and Eve walked with God in the garden. They were both naked, and they were not ashamed (see Gen. 2:25). The destructive power of unhealthy shame visited humanity as a result of the Fall into disobedience. Gershen Kaufman powerfully writes:

Shame is the affect which is the source of many complex and disturbing inner states: depression, alienation, self-doubt, isolating loneliness, paranoid and schizoid phenomena, compulsive disorders, splitting of self, perfectionism, a deep sense of inferiority, inadequacy or failure, the so-called borderline conditions and disorders of narcissism.[vii]

The condition of Adam and Eve after their disobedience to God portrays a depiction of the human condition hiding from God and each other in utter shame. Sin brings shame. Shame brings the false self. In our wounded nature, we seek out wholeness in false ways. The false sense of self exists apart from union with God. It bears an image born out of sin rather than an image born out of God. Victimized by shame, we think we can walk in another's truth. But cut off from our healthy self-image in God, we can only desperately grasp at a mere vestige of freedom.

For the past 15 years I have worked at the Laver. As a clinical psychologist, I have had the privilege of professionally working thousands of hours with my patients. Most have been born-again believers who are struggling with their own wounded nature. Many have been abused victims. Sitting in my office I see them twice victimized. They are victimized by their abuser and victimized by their response to their abuse. In their broken state without recourse to justice, comfort, and release of pain, they hide the wound; they disengage with life; they alienate themselves, and they flounder in the pain of shame.

This is a paralyzing condition that can cause dissociative identity disorders. With all trust in fellow man broken, a cutting off of one's emotional life often results. Other times one can harbor deep-seated feeling of hatred at self and others. The perception of a God who wasn't there to protect them may leave them offended and angry.

John Bevere warns of the importance of our response when offended when he says in his book *The Bait of Satan* (Creation House, 1994), "One of the enemy's most deadly and deceptive traps...is the trap of offense. It imprisons countless Christians, severs relationships and widens the existing breaches between us." He goes on to say,

An offended brother or sister is harder to win than a fortified city. The strong cities had walls around them. These walls were the city's assurance of protection. We construct walls when we are hurt to safeguard our hearts and prevent any future wound. We become selective, denying entry to all we fear will hurt us.[viii]

An elder mentor of mine lost his 20 year-old son to suicide. He went to his son's college apartment at the University of Pennsylvania, and found his body hanging in the bathroom. I said to him, "Why did the Lord allow this to happen?" He turned to me quickly, pointed his finger in my face, and said, "Don't ever ask God why!" He told me he cut his son's body down, held him in his arms, thanked God for his life, and then offered him back to his Heavenly Father.

Our tragedies and disappointments must be viewed in a divine perspective that will draw us to God. These kinds of events force us on our knees. We need to hold on to God rather than push Him away. We must resist the temptation to blame God for not preventing the tragedy. We pray for the grace to trust God even when we do not understand.

To do otherwise is to go down a slippery slope that will lead to hardness of heart. Walls of protection develop keeping trespassers out. Walls of protection keep love and intimacy from entering. People who follow this slippery slope harden their hearts. Years of practice leave them as expert builders of these walls. All of these responses to the abuse and injustice are simply people's attempt to survive.

God offers a much better solution to the problem. Victims need not be victims anymore. Victims need not define themselves by personal sin or by the sin against them. The cross of Jesus disarms the powers and authorities of evil with all their deception. *"He made a public spectacle of them, triumphing over them by the cross"* (Col. 2:15). One's pathogenic relationship with a false identity gives way to something whole in Jesus Christ. Issues of abandonment, rejection, insecurity, and self-hatred are washed in the waters of Christ's true love.

The provision of the Laver is large enough for our most pressing needs. The water that came down from the Heavens to fill the Laver was a continual provision by God. The living waters of Jesus will never run out. There is always more water available for the cleansing of the hidden parts in our minds and spirits. These hidden, secretive parts need not defile us any longer. God brings provision designed to wash over our painful memories and shameful bondage.

The Woman at the Well

Jesus is represented as our Laver in the account of the Samaritan woman at the well. In this beautiful story Jesus goes out of His way for a woman living out of her false sense of self. We don't know much about her history, but it should suffice to say that like anyone coming from a family life that was seriously lacking, she struggled with shame. Jesus encounters her at the well of Jacob and manages to turn her attention from well water to something deeper. Jesus says, *"If you knew the gift of God and who it is that asks you for a drink, you would have asked Him and He would have given you living water"* (John 4:10).

Jesus is asking for her whole being. He wants to fill her with His grace. He gently disposes her toward receiving Him. He gradually transforms each person He loves. Each part of the transformation is a further invitation rather than an imposition. His goal is to have the woman gaze into the deepest well of His eyes.

This is where she will be transformed. In the amazement of the totality of endless love, the woman will come to a place where she can give up her defenses. The fulfillment of love that she so desperately sought in all the wrong places gives way to the real and lasting thing. Her repetitious thirst to fill her love followed the natural tendencies of her flesh prior to this most holy encounter. Her wounded soul could never attain what she so compulsively pursued.

Jesus deftly calls her out of her shame by graciously exposing her places of shame.

He told her, "Go, call your husband and come back." "I have no husband," she replied. Jesus said to her, "You are right when you say you have no husband. The fact is, you have had five husbands, and the man you now have is not your husband. What you have just said is quite true." (John 4:16-18).

Fear of exposure lies in the pit of shame. Here is where vulnerability must be unearthed. Jesus, the master psychotherapist, enters into a place heretofore forbidden. Shame holds her back from intimacy with God. It keeps her at a distance from God.

Fears cripple and cause one to cower and even lie to oneself about the truth. When divine love shows up, it manifests an incomparable ability to disarm without condemnation. The gentle reminder of the truth Jesus gives her through word of knowledge stirs little reproach or threat. *"A bruised reed He will not break, and a smoldering wick He will not snuff out"* (Isa. 42:3).

By reminding her of her five marriages and her current affair, Jesus has led her to the place of repentance. She begins to see the vain attempt made on her part to fulfill what only God can fulfill. She accepts the gift of forgiveness, love, and living water all wrapped up in the person of the Lord. With the woman's shame removed, it becomes the essential component to her testimony. The very thing she once so carefully kept hidden, she now shouts from the housetops because He has set her free.

Then, leaving her water jar, the woman went back to the town and said to the people, "Come, see a man who told me everything I ever did. Could this be the Christ?" They came out of the town and made their way toward him. (John 4:28-30).

Putting down the water jar meant putting down her former life. In her excitement she had much more important things to be about then simply collecting water in a jar. A high power and presence moves her; stirred by a voice that would not be stilled, she hurries back to tell the very people she once tried to avoid. Twice each day, morning and evening, women came to the well outside the city to draw water for their daily household needs. The Samaritan woman in our story came at noon likely to avoid being talked about by the other women. She knew she was of ill repute. Any reminder of the state of her condition was like pouring salt into a wound. She recognized that her testimony about Jesus might fall short, so she told everybody to come and see Him.

Perhaps our prayer might be to let go of the water jar in our life that we use to define us. In reality it may be an encumbrance and the very thing that separates us from the living waters of God.

Like the story of the Samaritan woman at the well, the Bible is full of examples of broken people touched by the hand of mercy and love. His touch, like no other touch, can take someone abandoned, rejected, or lost, and make them His very best friend. When injustices come your way, when you get what you don't deserve, when all is unfair and even cruel, recognize that there is One who will never leave you or forsake you. When tragedy strikes and troubles are staring you in the face, it is easy to turn away from God, but it is easier to turn to God.

Family Rejection

Think about the biblical account of Samuel the prophet sent to the house of Jesse to anoint one of his sons as king. Jesse lined up seven sons for the prophet's inspection. He turned to Jesse and said "Don't you have anymore sons?" Jesse replied there was one more tending the sheep. He was brought into the house, and God told Samuel, *"Arise, anoint him; for this is he. Then Samuel took the horn of oil and anointed him in the midst of his brothers; and the Spirit of the Lord came upon David from that day forward"* (1 Sam. 16:12b-13). Here one reads that David wasn't even counted by Jesse as a son. Seven brothers were lined up for the honor, yet Jesse didn't give David the possibility to be selected as next king of Judah. David was virtually rejected and left out by his father. Although the world didn't count him, God counted him.

It doesn't matter if you came from a family in which you were rejected. It doesn't really matter that you were abandoned. If you came from a dysfunctional family that mistreated you or didn't love you, that family might be the very thing used by God to drive you toward His loving arms. God's love is all one needs. God moves through powerlessness to power, through weakness to strength, through smallness to greatness, through dependence to freedom.

God is found in weakness and vulnerability. One cannot come to God while striving for greatness, success, influence, and power. One can only come to God as a child in need. *"Unless you change and become like little children, you will never enter the Kingdom of Heaven."* (Matt. 18:3). The way to remain mentally and emotionally healthy is to remain a child at heart.

The good news of Jesus is not only the provision made to have our sin cancelled, but also the provision made whereby redemption is provided to restore us from the consequences of sin. To become a believer by accepting the gift of God's forgiveness for one's sins is to accept salvation. This change in the heart does not instantaneously change everything else.

Becoming a Christian does not immediately restore us to the image of God. We must be gradually transformed by the renewing of the mind. Salvation then puts us on the road to recovery. Our psychological and personality transformation varies as we walk in the renewing of the mind according to Christ. Our individual personality will likely remain stable over time since God does not come to destroy our unique person. Personal healing and restoration occur in the process of renewal in Him. This is what Paul writes to new believers,

You were taught, with regard to your former way of life, to put off your old self, which is being corrupted by its deceitful desires; to be made new in the attitude of your minds; and to put on the new self, created to be like God in true righteousness and holiness (Eph. 4:22-24).

Clearly, the essential work of God's plan takes place in the Outer Court ministry stations. These two stations use both blood and water to bring about change in humankind. As Jesus hung on the cross for us, the lance pierced His precious side. Blood and water flowed out from His side. The blood releases us from guilt, but the water frees us from shame. Both sin and iniquity are conquered in the Outer Court of the Tabernacle.

In our next chapter, we will move from the Outer Court of the Tabernacle to inside the Holy Place. So much can be said about what God has already provided, yet there is more with God. Those who are still hungry will follow the path, which leads to more of God. His invitation awaits us. Let us look into the part of the Tabernacle called the Holy Place.

PART TWO
STEPPING INTO POWER

CHAPTER SIX

GIFTED (THE GOLDEN LAMPSTAND)

The Nature of Holiness

In the Outer Court our focus has been on the removal of sin. In the Holy Place our emphasis will be on the way to holiness. Scripture says, *"As obedient children, do not conform to the evil desires you had when you lived in ignorance. But just as He who called you is holy, so be holy in all you do"* (1 Pet. 1:14-15).

Notice, God says, *"Be holy, as I am holy."* (1 Pet. 1:16). We recall from a study of the purpose of the Law that no one had the power to keep the Law. The Law was broken to reveal that no one had the power to keep it. God could not be encouraging us to keep a new morality since no one could keep the old morality. God is not advocating legalism, for God despises legalism. Legalism is a manifestation of the religious spirit, which is a great enemy of God.

The word "religion" in and of itself is not a pejorative word. However if we remember the way the Scribes and

Pharisees mistreated Jesus, one begins to understand what is meant by "religious spirit." The Scribes and Pharisees tried repeatedly to catch Jesus in defiance of the Law. They were full of pride and were smug in thinking that they were keeping to a "holy" life. The fact was that their hearts were far from God, and their pompous lives as religious men of God were nothing more than an empty sham. The hypocrisy of the Scribe and Pharisee is so potently described in the words of Jesus Himself in the Gospel.

Then Jesus said to the crowds and to his disciples: "The teachers of the law and the Pharisees sit in Moses' seat. So you must obey them and do everything they tell you. But do not do what they do, for they do not practice what they preach They tie up heavy loads and put them on men's shoulders, but they themselves are not willing to lift a finger to move them. Everything they do is done for men to see: They make their phylacteries wide and the tassels on their garments long; they love the place of honor at banquets and the most important seats in the synagogues; they love to be greeted in the marketplaces and to have men call them 'Rabbi'" (Matthew 23:1-7).

Jesus continues to berate these "religious" people with six "woes" against them calling the religious "blind guides, vipers, and serpents." The lifestyle of the "religious" person is a pious adherence to religious tradition. It has nothing to do with holiness. Their religious mentality is more sacred to them than what God might be doing today. The religious spirit will do anything it can to kill a move of God's Holiness in order to preserve its religious position.

The word of God teaches that we break the Law to expose our sin and our need for salvation. God is not encouraging us to try to become like Him. No amount of effort on our part would ever make us like God. Even though we may be covered by the sacrifice of the Brazen Altar, and washed by the water of the Brazen Laver, we could never be holy as the Lord our God is holy by performance and effort.

The answer to our dilemma lies in looking at the structure of the Tabernacle itself, and then in examining the three items of furniture in the Holy Place. The way to holiness comes through understanding the nature of the Holy Place. As one will come to see, the Holy Place is the place where God "gifts" for holiness. It is the place where God lavishly gifts us with holiness. Holiness then is a gift we receive from God.

Andrew Murray, in his classic work, *The Holiest of All* (Whitaker House, 1997), says the word *holiness* is one of the deepest in Scripture. It means a great deal more than separated or consecrated to God. Murray writes, "Holiness is the deepest mystery of God's Being, the wonderful union of His righteousness and His love."[ix] Therefore, God's very essence is to be holy. He exudes and emanates holiness. He touches us, and we are holy.

Righteousness is never a work we do. It is not something we can imitate. There are those who naively teach that holiness is something we choose. This is only partially true. It may begin with a deliberate choice, but the change in us depends solely on God's gift. Along with choosing good and avoiding evil, we need the grace or touch of God's Holiness before we become holy. God rewards us choosing good and denying our flesh with a touch of His very essence. Without His divine touch, we find ourselves caught up in extrinsic works, which have no intrinsic origin. These types of works are works of the flesh and products of the flesh. God's word says, *"Be holy, for I am holy"* (1 Pet. 1:16). To be holy reaches the essence of being. It is not simply an attribute that we wear at times and not at other times. It is not something that we try to do and find ourselves succeeding sometimes and failing at other times. Holiness is righteous. It does not fail. It is godliness. It does not fail.

Murray says, "To be holy is to be in fellowship with God, possessed of Him." God does not say that holiness comes out of choosing and trying harder the next time around. If this were true it would be a work of the flesh. The truth is that the righteous work flows out of change that occurs in our being due to being in fellowship with God.

It is here in the Holy Place of the Tabernacle that the Holy Spirit, who especially bears the name Holy, becomes the bearer of holiness to all who desire more of God. As our human fleshly tendencies bow humbly before God's greatness, the Holy Spirit shares the greatness of His holiness.

Brilliance in the Temple

The rectangular shaped Tabernacle, which housed the Holy Place, was 30 feet long and only 15 feet wide. The

Holy of Holies was 15 square feet. The heavy veil divided the two separate chambers. Light emanated from the 125 pound golden Lampstand. Its brilliance provided lighting for the entire Holy Place.

It was a seven-branched candlestick, with a central shaft larger than the other six branches. The artwork on the candlestick crafted the three stages of the almond: the bud, the flower, and the ripened fruit. Each branch had three complete sets, making a grand total of nine. The central shaft had four sets of the three stages of the almond carved on it. The significance of the *almond tree*, which means, "expecting," is that it is the first tree to come to life after the winter passes. The almond tree survives the death of winter and comes to life in spring. It even bears first fruit before any other tree shows life. God's word predicted, *"A shoot will come up from the stump of Jesse; from his roots a Branch will bear fruit"* (Isa. 11:1). At Calvary this prediction would come to pass, and He would become *"the first fruits of those who have fallen asleep"* (1 Cor. 15:20).

When John had his vision of Heaven on the island of Patmos, he saw that *"before the throne, seven lamps were blazing. These are the seven spirits of God"* (Rev. 4:5). Seven is the spiritual number for perfection symbolizing the Holy Spirit. The Spirit of the Lord is the central shaft of the candlestick while the three branches on either side represent His titles. *"And the Spirit of the Lord will rest on Him, the spirit of wisdom and understanding, the spirit of counsel and power, the spirit of knowledge and of the fear of the Lord"* (Isa. 11:2).

The oil in the Lampstand also typifies the Holy Spirit. Oil was used in the anointing of a person called to perform a special task. It was the anointing from God that enabled the person to accomplish the special task. The person aside from the anointing could not accomplish the task. The anointing from the oil brings the power, which enables. God gave the Law to Moses under the Old Covenant. The Holy Spirit is the lawgiver under the New Covenant.

For what the law was powerless to do in that it was weakened by the sinful nature, God did by sending his own Son in the likeness of sinful man to be a sin offering. And so He condemned sin in sinful man, in order that the righteous requirements of the law might be fully met in us, who do not live according to the sinful nature but according to the Spirit (Romans 8:3-4).

We are now enabled to keep the Law of Moses through the convincing power of the Holy Spirit. God's word tells of the day when the anointing would break the yoke of bondage. It speaks of a time when humankind's burden would be destroyed. *"It shall come to pass in that day that his burden will be taken away from your shoulder, and his yoke from your neck, and the yoke will be destroyed because of the anointing oil"* (Isa. 10:27 NKJV).

The passage speaks of the bondage placed by the devil on the human race. The yoke is broken through the power of the Holy Spirit. God's Spirit abides in us. His power lives in the bodies of those who believe. His power is made evident in those released in the anointing of the Holy Spirit.

This power or anointing is not simply a footnote in the sacred Scriptures. The promise of the coming of the Holy Spirit is the fulfillment of major prophecies from the Old Testament. Jeremiah announced:

"The time is coming," declares the Lord, "when I will make a new covenant with the house of Israel and with the house of Judah. This is the covenant I will make with the house of Israel after that time," declares the Lord. "I will put my law in their minds and write it on their hearts. I will be their God, and they will be my people" (Jeremiah 31:31,33).

Ezekiel also prophesied:

I will show the holiness of My great name, which has been profaned among the nations...I will give you a new heart and put a new spirit in you; I will remove from you your heart of stone and give you a heart of flesh. And I will put My Spirit in you and move you to follow my decrees and be careful to keep my laws. (Ezekiel 36:23a,26-27).

The promise echoed in the words of Jeremiah and Ezekiel came to fulfillment on the day of Pentecost as tongues of fire descended upon the 120 in the Upper room. God's Holy Spirit was now poured out on all flesh. It was the Holy Spirit in them, which transformed them from timidity to a sound mind. The Holy Spirit poured into them power and authority. The Book of Acts chronicles the signs and wonders of the apostles going forth in great boldness in the name of the Lord.

The apostle Paul's prayer for the Church stated, *"I bow my knees before the Father…that He would grant you, according to the riches of His glory, to be strengthened with might through His Spirit in the inner man"* (Eph. 3:14,16 NKJV). Paul's prayer for the early Church is a prayer for "more of Him." Guy Chevreau writes in his book *Pray with Fire* (Harper Collins, 1995) that the Greek in this verse literally means, "power to become mighty through the Spirit of Him in the inward man." He goes on to say this is not about self-actualization; this is not might in and for us. The power and anointing is given by God, and is poured into our being. We cannot self-actualize to grow in the power of the Holy Spirit. It is a gift, which comes to indwell in those who desire *"More."*[x]

So, we are released in the gift of the Holy Spirit when we come into the Holy Place and stand before the Golden Lampstand. Recall that the Lampstand was patterned after the revelation in Isaiah 11:2. The gift of the Spirit brings supernatural charisms enabling us to bring *"the Spirit of the Lord"* into situations.

The charisms are categorized into three groups: (1) the wisdom gifts, (2) the power gifts, and (3) the prophetic gifts. For mainstream, classical Pentecostalism, the baptism in the Holy Spirit recorded in the Book of Acts is the second experience in the Christian journey. The first and essential experience is of course the acceptance of Jesus Christ as personal Savior in water baptism. Baptism brings true repentance for sin. This repentance makes way for regeneration in Christ. Some believe the baptism in the Holy Spirit can come simultaneous with, rather than subsequent to, conversion.

Classical Pentecostals believe the full release of the Holy Spirit, however, comes with the baptism by fire. Evidence of receiving the baptism of the Holy Spirit comes with the charismatic manifestation called *glossolalia*, or speaking in tongues. Along with speaking in tongues, other gifts come forth with the release of the Holy Spirit in a believer's life. The wisdom gifts include wisdom, knowledge, and discerning of spirits; the power gifts include faith, healing, and miracles; and the word gifts include tongues, the interpretation of tongues, and prophecy. These spiritual gifts empower the believer to move in a supernatural way (see 1 Cor. 12:8-11).

There are those in the Church who would disagree with the classical understanding of the gifts of the Holy Spirit. For example, some Evangelicals don't believe the supernatural gifts are for today. They rather see the gifts as operative only during the time frame of the apostles. Other Christians believe the baptism in the Holy Spirit comes simultaneous with, rather than subsequent to, conversion. Tongues may or may not accompany the baptism. Gifts may appear even if a person has not had a separate experience of the baptism, but rather simply is open to the Holy Spirit.

The Book of Acts is clear on the distinction between water baptism and the baptism of the Holy Spirit. Luke records the anomalous situation of the mission to Samaria. Here, men already water baptized in the name of the Lord Jesus were prayed over by Peter and John for the baptism of the Holy Spirit (see Acts 8:9-19). Conclusively, it is the baptism of Jesus which should provide the model for Christian initiation. Jesus believed in a baptism for repentance and a baptism of empowerment. Even John realized the distinctive elements of repentance and power when he said, *"I baptize you with water. But one more powerful than I will come, the thongs of whose sandals I am not worthy to untie. He will baptize you with the Holy Spirit and with fire"* (Luke 3:16). It is both the forgiveness and power of the Holy Spirit that are the vital factors in Christian initiation.

A Willing Lampstand

Let me use my own story as an illustration of this truth. Bear in mind that at this point in my life I was baptized and raised in a Christian family. I so loved God that I dedicated my life to His work . I was ordained and commissioned as a Roman Catholic priest. Shortly after the time of my desperate need for more of God as a parish priest, a small group of people began to pray in the rectory basement. I had just cried out to God, "God, if you don't do something in my life and ministry, I will have to quit this work." He truly hears the cry of the desperate heart. This desperation or dryness in me led to God's wooing me deeper once more.

Since the group met in my house it was next to impossible to avoid what they were doing. Besides, I believed I had a responsibility to the church to check them out. They would sit in a circle and pray to Jesus as if He were present in the room. They had no formal prayers, or prayer books. They prayed spontaneously and informally in a manner that I was unaccustomed. The leader of the group invited me to teach them. He wouldn't give me a topic to speak about, rather he told me to let the Holy Spirit lead me. I really didn't know what he was talking about. I did, however, spend an enormous amount of time in prayer for this little ten-minute teaching. The reason I prepared for this teaching in such a diligent way was, quite frankly, out of fear. They seemed to know Jesus better than I did!

Following much deliberation, I decided to talk about God's presence in creation. They had no idea what I was going to speak about. I felt very insecure as I approached them armed with my Bible, concordance, and reams of notes. We sat down as the leader led in prayer. He said, "Thank you, heavenly Father, for this beautiful day. Thank you for the birds of the sky and the fish of the sea. Thank you for creation." We then sang a song on creation. Someone read an account on creation from the Book of Genesis. This was getting to be very strange as I squirmed in my seat. Another person read Psalm 104, the creation psalm. The final clincher came when somebody read from the Book of Colossians, which was the text upon which I based my teaching. I nearly jumped out of my skin.

Did you ever feel like God set you up? This is how I felt. God orchestrated this entire evening to let me know that He was for real. He was present in His creation; He was present in that room in His Spirit. He convinced me that night that I needed a personal encounter with the living God like these people had. Although I spent years in seminary, although I was ordained a priest, it didn't make any difference. Each person needs to be empowered by the Holy Spirit. The group offered to lay hands on me to pray for the baptism of the Holy Spirit that night. I was too overwhelmed with what had just taken place and declined their offer.

I attended a "Life in the Spirit" seminar series, which led up to the baptism of fire. Let me tell you about that night November 5, 1975, which I would come to see as the greatest night of my life. Three people laid hands on me and prayed a simple prayer asking Jesus to baptize me in the Holy Spirit. They prayed in their prayer language, and my body began to tremble and shake. I shook and shook and shook. My body went into convulsions as I shook off the pew. I screamed out for it to stop, but it only went on and on. Power went through me like waves of electricity. This went on for perhaps a half-hour to an hour. I really don't know how long it continued. The prayer team looked scared and left me there alone. They didn't know what to do since they had never seen such a thing. The shaking began to subside, and I began to cry out of the deepest recesses of my being.

I recall saying quietly, "My God, You have been here all this time, and I never really knew it like I now know it. You who are so great are at the same time so close." I felt His love consume me. I felt Him cleanse me of all former hurt by His consuming passionate love. Now God was real in my life. He was more real than anyone or anything. My categories for thinking about Him were totally changed in a moment of time.

There were 120 people baptized in the Spirit that night in my church. This is precisely the same number of people gathered in the upper room on the day of Pentecost. The number has great significance. In Genesis 6:3, Noah finished construction of the ark after 120 years. This marked the end of the age of man and the workings of the flesh, and the beginning of the age of the Spirit. God said, *"My Spirit shall not strive with man forever, for he is truly flesh; yet his days shall be 120 years"* (NKJV).

The night of my baptism by fire left me with a tangible anointing all around me. I knew it was the cloud of God's glory. I was walking in another dimension. It was the closest thing I could imagine to Heaven. The presence of God was all about me. The following day I searched to see if anyone else had ever seen such a thing. Many said they came into a new relationship with God and even received the gift of tongues. But as wonderful as these experiences seemed, no one could identify what happened to me. Eventually, I researched revival testimonials. I came across the story of evangelist Charles G. Finney from the nineteenth century.

Charles G. Finney

Finney faced the question of leaving ministry because he didn't see the power of the gospel. If he could not have the Jesus of the gospel, he would leave the pastorate and would pursue a worldly course of life. He decided to cry out to God for more. Finney writes in his autobiography (*Charles G. Finney* by Helen Wessel, Bethany House, 1977):

As I turned and was about to take a seat by the fire, I received a mighty baptism of the Holy Spirit. Without any expectation of it, without ever having the thought in my mind that there was such a thing for me, without any memory of ever hearing the thing mentioned by any person in the world, the Holy Spirit descended upon me in a manner that seemed to go through body, soul and me.

I could feel the impression, like a wave of electricity, going through me and through me. Indeed, it seemed to come in waves of liquid love, for I could not express it any other way. It seemed like the very breath of God. I can distinctly remember that it seemed to fan me like immense wings. No words can express the wonderful love that was spread abroad in my heart. I wept aloud with joy and love. I literally bellowed out the unspeakable overflow of my heart. These waves came over me, and over me, and over me, one after another, until I remember crying out, "I shall die if these waves continue to pass over me." I said, "Lord, I cannot bear anymore." Yet I had no fear of death.

How long I continued in this state, with the baptism continuing to roll over me and going through me, I do not know. But I know it was late in the evening when a member of the choir came into my office to see me. He found me in a state of loud weeping, and said to me, "Mr. Finney, what's wrong with you?" I could not answer for some time. He then said, "Are you in pain?" I gathered myself up as best I could, and replied, "No, but I'm so happy that I cannot live."[xi]

Finney's words brought so much peace and satisfaction to me. I had an experience with God identical to his experience. We both found ourselves immersed in the baptism by fire. The morning after the experience the fire of God was still upon me. The anointing was all over me. My body was burning with a fire that came from within me. I'd go to bed at night, and my hands would burn night after night with this fire within me. The baptism by fire consumed me like I was a burning bush. I had no control over it. I knew things about people's lives that I had no idea about. Words would simply and effortlessly fall into my mind about people. I knew what people's sins were by simply looking at them. I knew sins, but not in a judgmental way. My lines for the confessional were endless as I heard confessions for 5 to 6 hours on Saturday. People came just to hear the priest who could tell them their sins before they could tell him.

God had done a shaking in me. I thought of the word of God in the Book of Hebrews, *"'Once more I will shake not only the earth but also the heavens.'* The words 'once more' indicate the removing of what can be shaken—that is, created things—*so that what cannot be shaken may remain"* (Heb. 12:26b-27). Our God is a consuming fire. All flesh must be consumed before Him. John the Baptist spoke of this fire when he said, *"I baptize you with water for repentance. But after me will come one who is more powerful than I, whose sandals I am not fit to carry. He will baptize you with the Holy Spirit and with fire"* (Matt. 3:11).

I remember one humorous story about our school children coming over for confession. My hands were hot as usual. Twelve hundred and fifty children needed confession. As the first child came into the confessional room, he sat down in a chair opposite me. He told me his sins. I stretched out my hand to bless him, when all of a sudden he fell unconscious in the chair. I had never heard about anyone "slain in the Spirit." So, I picked him up and laid him in the corner of the room. I wasn't thinking that he had fainted. I could feel the power go out from my hand. I knew God was in charge. I signaled Sister to send in the next child for confession.

Instantly the next child is unconscious in the chair again from the power from my hand. I laid her beside the boy. This went on with two more children until I ran out of room, and Sister's curiosity peaked wondering why her children were not coming out of the confessional. It is all about the power of the Holy Spirit!

Miraculous Power

I began praying with the sick in the area hospital. The family of a woman lying in bed with terminal cancer asked for prayer. She was put on morphine to kill the pain of the cancer. The staff at the hospital knew she was about to die. I laid hands on the woman, and cast out the spirit of death and cancer in the name of Jesus. She got up out of her deathbed, and a day later was discharged without any cancer. Word of this miracle spread through the hospital. The woman testified at my first miracle service about two months later. I found myself doing what Jesus did in His public ministry. No longer did I have to resort to a feeble blessing or only words that were powerless. Now, I could see the mighty works of God healing the sick in the name of Jesus.

God's word became very clear in my spirit from that time forward. I believe He told me it was not enough to see His people healed here and there. He wanted me to hold a gathering where people could bring the sick and have prayer for healing. This healing service was announced at our ever-growing prayer group. The prayer group became the largest in the nation in a Catholic church. The first night of the healing service brought in over 1,000 people. The second month was close to 2,000 people. The Lord outdid Himself meeting the needs of the people. He was faithful to show up every time. It was glorious. People began to gather two hours before the doors opened to get a seat to be with Jesus. Buses brought groups of people from far away distances. The parking situation became a problem in the township. These problems occurred because so many people were coming to church. They knew God was in the house.

Following the first night's service, the Lord spoke something wonderful to me. He said, "Thank you, Frank, for giving me the opportunity to show My people how much I love them." In other words God was saying, "Just give Me a chance to do what I can do. Give Me the opportunity to heal, and I will heal." The key here is that we did not go forth in our own power. The anointing alone breaks the yoke of the devil.

Signs and wonders occurred at every meeting. Let me share with you some of the healing and miracles I witnessed to build up your faith.

One woman came down the church aisle with her seeing-eye dog. She was totally blind from birth. The first thing that happened was the German shepherd was slain in the Spirit before the woman reached me. All watching were in shock. One of my assistants thought this happened to protect me from the dog if it got upset when the woman was slain in the Spirit. However, I think God rather wanted the woman to let go of everything she was dependent upon before she came to Him. God thinks of everything. I laid hands on the woman's eyes, and the power of God was present to heal. She opened her eyes and looked around the room. She said she saw light and shadows. I recalled Jesus praying with the man born blind. The blind man began to see people who "looked like walking trees." So I prayed a second time just as He did. This time she saw in color with clarity! Tears rolled down this elderly woman's cheeks as she thanked God for the miracle she received.

Another remarkable miracle occurred in a ten year-old boy who had no eardrum in his right ear. Surgery was scheduled the following day to graft a plastic eardrum into the ear. During the service I shook hands with him, and he immediately heard a popping sound in his right ear. The boy tugged at his mother saying he could now hear. The next day the surgeon confirmed his ability to hear, and admitted God had given the boy a brand new eardrum.

I prayed with a metropolitan, air-traffic, helicopter pilot. The pilot crashed and broke his neck and his back in multiple places. I had him take off his brace and prayed. His 6'4" frame crashed to the floor. He arose from the floor completely restored with no pain.

I prayed for a young woman who ended up paraplegic from a terrible car accident. I have seen people come out of wheelchairs because of arthritis, rheumatism, osteoporosis, and old age. Never before had I seen this kind of miracle. One woman's spinal cord had severed in the car accident two years previous. I laid my right hand on the upper part of her spine. God knit the spine together as the heat was released from my hand. I then took her by the hand, and told her in the name of Jesus to stand up and walk. Her legs had atrophied, but her faith was great. She got up and walked with me about 30 feet across the front of the church. Later in the year, I married her and became her husband. She walked down the aisle with her father.

I have seen the Lord heal paralyzed hands and arms and lengthen legs. The most remarkable miracle of this sort I witnessed occurred when I had a word of knowledge about someone with a foot problem. The Spirit of the Lord led me through the crowd to the afflicted person. It was amazing to know who it was that needed healing. As I approached the woman, I heard a crash to the floor. There in the distance was the woman, slain in the Spirit. I looked down at her foot, and noticed she had a specially designed shoe for a clubfoot. I had some people take the shoe off. I took the stump of a foot into my two hands and prayed. The heat from my hands grew enormously hot. The power of God poured out for the lady. Things shifted around, and bones crackled. Ligaments moved as well as bones. My focus remained in prayer until the Lord led me to do otherwise. Her toes were all tucked under her foot like petrified wood. As the energy went out of me the bottom of the foot softened. Then all the toes shot open simultaneously then closed again. Again the toes opened, supple and healed. God gave this woman a new foot.

I have had the privilege to see God heal cancer dozens of times. I've seen extreme fevers break instantly by the anointing of God. God has used me to heal diabetes, lupus, kidney disease, and heart disease numerous times. I have seen God touch backs and necks in seconds. People have come on respirators and oxygen tanks because of emphysema and lung disorders. God has healed them immediately. I prayed with a mentally challenged school aged girl. She was re-tested at her school because of recognizable behavioral changes. Her IQ changed from 65 to a normal 100.

One astounding miracle occurred when a young mother brought an infant before the crowds of people for a miracle. The baby's head was hydrocephalic. I laid my hands on the head and prayed to the Lord to take away the water from the brain. The head size went down, and down. Where the water went, I don't know. God did another miracle.

Not all healing is physical in nature. God likewise freed many from spiritual, emotional, and mental bondage. I recall a persistent woman literally pulling at me at the close of a service. She pressed in until the Lord touched her. Both of her hands were crippled from arthritis. I spoke a word of knowledge to her that she harbored jealousy at her sister and anger toward her deceased mother. I told this 65 year-old woman that she had held resentment in her heart all these years. Her sister stood beside her as she asked the Lord for forgiveness. I then prayed and said, "In the name of Jesus stretch out your hand." Immediately, her hands opened free from all effects of arthritis. I could relate many other stories about healing from depression, anxiety, and deep scars of abuse. I've seen the Lord set people free from the bondage of addiction to drugs, alcohol, and prescription drugs.

Angelic Agents

I just got back into ministry a couple of years ago. One of my first healing meetings occurred in Nashville, Tennessee. I pointed out a 15 year-old girl during the service. She had a huge goiter growing on the left side of her neck. I told her God was healing her. She fell crashing to the floor with the power of these words. I walked over to her, and placed my hand on her neck. I cursed the growth, and immediately it went down, down, down, and left. Her father stood over her crying at what God did. He had two hearing aids in his ears. He told me artillery fire damaged his ears while serving in war. I told him to take out the hearing aids. I prayed and God instantly opened both ears.

While this was going on a little girl perhaps three or four years old dressed in a pretty white dress danced. She tugged on her mommy and yelled, "Mommy, Mommy, look at the man up front." The mother leaned down and told her that was the preacher. But the little girl replied, "No, not him. I mean the beautiful man behind him." Times are here already when the young will see visions. She saw a beautiful angel ministering healing and miracles beside me.

In 1975, the Spirit of God told me that a special angel would go out with me to heal the sick. He told me the angel's name is Raphael. I didn't think much on the name until years later. It occurred to me that the prefix "rapha" means healing, and the suffix "el" means God. His name is "I am the God who heals thee." The Bible teaches that God uses ministering angels to heal in the name of the Lord Jesus.

As we get hold of this message, we will understand that the unseen is more real than the tangible and the sensate. As we perceive that the invisible is more real than that which is visible to us, then we will open up to the things of the Spirit. The presence of God includes His angelic choirs of angels. As we go out, we go out accompanied by angels from God's portals of glory.

The Lord is combing the earth in search of willing vessels to be used for healing. Some individual gifts may be singular in scope, but the call to heal in His name is still universal. There is nothing in this world more satisfying or more exciting than to be used by God for someone's healing. We are called to be His hands, His heart, and His voice to this dying world. For if we are not His hands used to touch the sick, then whose hands is He to use? If we are not His heart of love and mercy, then whose heart is He to use? If we are not His voice to announce the good news, then whose voice is He to use? Some believe the age of miracles is over and ended with the death of the last apostle. But for those touched with the fire of God, they know God is waiting to raise new vessels to carry His banner out to the nations.

I choose to place a heavy emphasis on the gifts of healing, faith, and miracles because Jesus Himself placed a heavy emphasis on them. During His public ministry Jesus relied on the Holy Spirit to anoint Him with the power to heal, and again, the Holy Spirit continued to place a high premium on the power gifts during the early spread of the gospel in the Book of Acts. This in no way is meant to minimize any of the other gifts of the Holy Spirit. These gifts are as necessary today as they were then as a proclamation of good news and as a demonstration of God's power over evil.

Most important to personal growth and character development is the fruit of the Holy Spirit. It is essential to remember that the Holy Spirit does not bring us instantaneous sanctity, but rather the power and ability to change. The power of the Holy Spirit enables us to mature in holiness. Paul reminds us to *"live by the Spirit, and you will not gratify the desires of the sinful nature. For the sinful nature desires what is contrary to the Spirit, and the Spirit what is contrary to the sinful nature"* (Gal. 5:16-17). Paul goes on to further say, *"the acts of the sinful nature are obvious...but the fruit of the Spirit is love, joy, peace, patience, kindness, goodness, faithfulness, gentleness and self-control"* (Gal. 5:19,22-23).

This "conversion of the flesh" for most of us is a process of walking out the holiness. Our sinful nature doesn't always die readily. We generally need to call upon God's grace to overcome our sinful behavior.

Both the gifts and the fruit of the Holy Spirit come out of the deeper relationship you now have with the lover of your soul. It is here in the Holy Place of the Tabernacle that we begin to unearth these deeper treasures of God. It is wonderful to know that our God makes provision for us in the Holy Place to discover the beauty of the Holy Spirit at work in us.

CHAPTER SEVEN

TEAM PLAYERS (THE TABLE OF SHOWBREAD)

A description of the Table of Showbread is recorded in Exodus 25:30. God tells Moses to *"put the bread of the presence on this table to be before Me at all times."* The word *showbread* means "face bread or bread of the presence." The loaves of bread were set before the presence of God as a meal offering (see Lev. 24:8). The showbread consisted of 12 loaves of unleavened bread made of very fine flour and baked in an oven. Each Sabbath, fresh manna is placed on the table and sprinkled with frankincense. The priests ate the old bread. The 12 cakes were made of two-tenth deal of flour. This double-portion of flour is symbolic of Jesus, the Bread of Life. The fine flour was ground down to eliminate lumps. The loaves are placed in two rows of six each on the table. This signifies that each tribe and all men are equal before the presence of God. None is above or below another. The bread was to sit in the presence of God for a week. During this time the bread absorbed the presence of

God, and then was consumed by the priests who took on more of God's life through the bread of His presence.

The Object of the Game

There is a board game that I liked to play as a young boy called "Risk," which is manufactured by Parker Brothers. The object of the game is to use your troops to conquer countries of the world. This is done by strategically moving your forces around the board as you defeat your enemies. The ultimate goal is to dominate the world. Whenever I played this game, I played for keeps. I took no captives. It is an extremely competitive game for all playing.

Recently, I was at a friend's house for a night of fun and relaxation. He brought out the game, "Risk," which a group of us began to play. Some 40 years had past since I played this game, so initially I was excited to join in. My memories were piqued by the colors of the countries of the world on the board. The military pieces energetically stimulated my mind, as I would have armies under my control and at my beckon call in just a few minutes. As the game progressed something was definitely wrong. It wasn't the game that had changed. The rules and regulations were just as I had left them 40 years ago. I looked at my close friends around the table, and everyone seemed to be having a good time. The change, I realized, had occurred in me. I could no longer muster up "the killer instinct." The competitive spirit was non-existent. I had no desire to conquer the world at the expense of my friendships. I knew this was "just" a game, but I also knew some things were more important to me than a game.

We are not in this world alone. God means for us to live and work together in harmony. Sometimes our needs and our desires must be put aside in order for a greater good to be accomplished. Sometimes one needs to look at the showbread to see what God would have one to do. The simple dictum "What would Jesus do?" is not such a bad reminder when considering the greater good at hand.

We might ask, "What is the object of the game?" "Does winning mean crushing anyone whom might stand in your way?" "Are there other possible meanings to winning at life?" These are existential questions that each one must ask and put value to in life. Choices are made and decisions reached contingent upon what one's basic goals for the game of life are.

If we reflect back to the Table of the Showbread, we will clearly see the highest priority placed on unity and equality. The golden precept, "Do unto others as you would have them do to you" immediately comes to mind. Let me put it this way: the Table of Showbread or "face bread" is a constant reminder that as we look to the face of Jesus, we are called to a design far greater than any one of the parts gathered around the Table. We will be sure to take the lead from God. All of the rest of us will only reach our final destination by insisting that we share each other's gifts and talents, while looking out for the weaker members among us along the way.

To run the race God sets before us requires that we assume His rules and regulations. It demands that we set before us His greater goals and definitions to life. We assimilate the presence of the Showbread as did the priests of the Old Testament. We lay aside our selfish, narcissistic nature as we feed on the Bread of Life.

Selfish Nature

Narcissism is a pervasive pattern of self-centeredness that is found in humans from the very beginning of life. One way to understand it is to realize a child sees the world only through its own eyes, and cannot be expected to take others' concerns into play. The child is interested in its self-preservation at all costs. The whole world revolves around whatever it needs whenever it needs them. Please understand that I love children, and find them to be creative, fun, and loving all at the same time. What I am referring to is a deeper psychological trait that rears its ugly face from time to time.

As the child develops and learns that it is important to interact with countless numbers of other people in order to exist harmoniously, the child tempers its basic selfishness to defer to the greater common good of the many.

In the Book of Genesis, we read:

So God created man in His own image, in the image and likeness of God He created Him. Male and female He created them. And God blessed them and said to them, "Be fruitful, multiply, fill the earth and subdue it. Have dominion over the fish of the sea, the birds of the air, and over every living creature that moves upon the earth (Genesis 1:27-28).

God allowed, encouraged, and even commanded man to have dominion over the earth and all that He created on it. This is a wonderful blessing of stewardship that God has entrusted us with. Yet, it should go without saying that man was not to have dominion over man. Man, both male and female, is made in the image of God. We are made out of the very substance of God, if you will. We are made in His image and likeness. He put His Spirit in us.

Everything else created in the earth is made out of the dust of the earth. Even our bodies are made out of the earth. But a vital difference separates us from the rest of living and non-living things. God placed something of Himself in man. Each person has an eternal value and worth that goes beyond whatever else is in creation. God has separated us from the rest of His creation, and has placed us above it, yet not above one another. This is why we are not to have dominion over each other. When man dominates another human being he violates the commands and Law of God.

Dominion of man over man spells abuse. It is a violation of natural law. It creates division, bigotry, hatred, war, racism, and sexism. It undermines the very fabric of mutual trust with suspicion and deception. It opens the door to manipulation and stifles the rights and dignity of humanity. It is the ultimate power trip to control. Its motivating force is greed and selfishness. It can destroy the world. The stark reality is that ugly blotches of sin cover the face of the world. Perhaps this is why I had trouble playing the board game that night. I'd rather be part of a team building some sensibility back into our world. I'd rather see myself spending my time building treasure that will be lasting than a kingdom that will eventually perish.

The Staff of Life

The Showbread was a foreshadowing of Jesus, the Bread of Life. This meant that the natural bread eaten as the staff of life would only bring temporary satisfaction. Whoever partook of Jesus would receive eternal life. Jesus, the Bread of Life, would provide a satisfaction better than anything in this world. *"Taste and see that the Lord is good"* (Ps. 34:8).

It is interesting to note that Abraham, Isaac, and Jacob were sojourners in the wilderness land. They foraged and hunted not unlike the modern day nomadic Lapp people. They moved with their herds from place to place. But God led the people of Israel into the Promised Land for His purposes. As the descendents of the Patriarchs continued to move about like a nomadic tribe of Bedouin herdsman, they eventually entered the Promised Land. Something unusual and dramatic happened here. They settled. This became a giant leap forward for humankind. The reason they decided to settle was because this land *"flowed with milk and honey"* (Exod. 33:3). The so-called milk and honey was tied to the grain.

The Fertile Crescent of the Middle East produced beautiful, hybrid wheat that one today knows better as bread wheat. Philosopher of science Jacob Bronowski, writes in the *Ascent of Man* (Little, Brown, and Company, 1973) that unlike other grains the children of Israel had seen this grain would not blow in the wind. Rather when the chaff would break off, the grain would fall exactly where it grew. "Suddenly, man and the plant have come together."[xii]

Humanity became tied to the land. This was a revolutionary step for humankind since an agricultural civilization now would come forth. The nomadic ways of the past would give way to the bright promise of living off the land. Why do I emphasize this development so much? I emphasize this development because the ability to settle created villages and cities. Villages and cities created an interconnected society, and this society needed a spirit of cooperation to progress and grow. Once again, it is the bread that reminds us of our need as a society to come around each other at the table of the Lord.

The tribes of Israel fought hard to get into the Fertile Crescent, which extended up and down the Mediterranean coastline, across the Anatolia Mountains, and then down toward the Tigris and Euphrates mountains. Joshua, as commander-in-chief of Israel, skillfully guided the people to their destination. Victory over the enemy is not something that Joshua could ever take for granted. One can never be presumptuous with God. Joshua realized this, and carefully crafted his strategies based on the directives of the Lord. He also subordinated himself to God's commands. He never thought too highly of himself. The Book of Joshua records the following account:

As Joshua approached the city of Jericho, he looked up and saw a man facing him with sword in hand. Joshua went up to him and asked, "Are you friend or foe?" "Neither one," he replied. "I am the commander of the Lord's army." At this, Joshua fell with his face to the ground in reverence. "I am at Your command," Joshua said, "What do you want your servant to do?" The commander of the Lord's army replied, "Take off your sandals, for this is holy ground." And Joshua did as he was told (Joshua 5:13-15 NLT).

The Lord's messenger instructed Joshua to enter the land, which God would give him, with due reverence for God, but also with due reverence for the land. Jericho was an oasis on the edge of a desert. Here one sees water and wheat coming together aplenty. If humans are ever to get along, then they would be wise to consider God, fellow man, and the land in that order. The sacredness of why we are here must impregnate our relationships with God, each other, and our earth. Without this sense of the sacred enriching of our choices, we are destined to rob, kill, and destroy.

The newly formed agricultural society spawned values that were healthy for fostering community. It taught the people values like the importance of having roots, cooperation, friendship, and family tradition. Many years later, our industrial and technological industries, although advancing society is some respects, have also served to further foster isolationism and individualism. Capitalism has further contributed to propaganda of commodity consumption. Materialism has become an end in itself, which leaves little to no room for spirituality. Is it any wonder that the face of family life has radically changed? The very essence of unity and equality is so difficult to maintain in a fragmented society.

Jim Goll writes in *Father Forgive Us* (Destiny Image, 1999), "America thrives on consumerism. Nationwide credit card debt has never been higher; nor has the incidence of personal bankruptcy. Our national debt (the highest ever) and uncontrolled deficit spending threaten to mortgage our children's tomorrow…whatever happened to honor, honesty, integrity, morality, ethics, and character? They have been sacrificed on the altar of ambition, greed, lust, and indulgence…America has a love affair with Mammon. We worship at his altar, commit our lives to the pursuit of his values, and seek to build our society and culture according to his standards."[xiii]

The New Commandment

But what are God's standards on which one might build something lasting and eternal? The night before Jesus died, He gathered together around the Table of Showbread with His closest friends. He told them, *"I give you a new commandment: Love one another; just as I have loved you, you also must love one another"* (John 13:34). To love others was not a new commandment for observant Jews (see Lev. 19:18), but to love as Jesus loved and whom Jesus loved was revolutionary. Jesus said, *"For I tell you that unless your righteousness surpasses that of the Pharisees and the teachers of the law, you will certainly not enter the Kingdom of Heaven"* (Matt. 5:20). Jesus is expecting more from those answering the call of love. Jesus revolutionized the meaning of "love" with His own sacrificial offering of His life. He interprets the meaning of "love" when he teaches:

One day an expert in religious law stood up to test Jesus by asking him this question: "Teacher, what must I do to receive eternal life?" Jesus replied, "What does the law of Moses say? How do you read it?" The man answered, "'You must love the Lord your God with all your heart, all your soul, all your strength, and all your mind.' And, 'Love your neighbor as yourself.'" "Right!" Jesus told him. "Do this and you will live!" (Luke 10:25-28 NLT).

This was no new revelation to the Hebrew people who were accustomed to reciting "the great commandment" from Deuteronomy 6:4-9 twice every day:

Hear, O Israel: The Lord our God, the Lord is One. Love the Lord your God with all your heart and with all your soul and with all your strength. These commandments that I give you today are to be upon your hearts. Impress them on your children. Talk about them when you sit at home and when you walk along the road, when you lie down and when you get up. Tie them as symbols on your hands and bind them on your foreheads. Write them on the doorframes of your houses and on your gates.

But notice the lawyer also follows the great commandment with a quote from Leviticus (see Lev. 19:18) on loving one's neighbor as oneself. This was done to try to trap Jesus into defining the word "neighbor," which has several meanings in the rabbinical literature. This is why the lawyer proceeds to ask, "And who is my neighbor?"

The lawyer wanted to know what definition Jesus subscribed to. Whatever Jesus subscribed to would by nature exclude another definition. Therefore, love would become exclusionary. Jesus, knowing the intent of the lawyer, chooses to reply by telling the story of the Good Samaritan.

Here we have the story of a man who while on a journey, was beaten and robbed by bandits. Three men came upon the wounded man on the road. One was a priest; the second was a Levite; and the third was a Samaritan. Both the priest and the Levite passed by on the other side. The Samaritan, however, felt compassion for the man. He cared for the man's needs. Jesus then posits the question back to the man, *"Which of these three do you think proved to be a neighbor to the man who fell into the robber's hands"* (Luke 10:36).

The parable has one central insight, namely, that love has no boundaries. Love cannot be defined because by nature it is limitless. As soon as one tries to define it like the lawyer, it becomes a sterile, closed ethic. Love is so much more than a mere duty. It must flow out of a place of compassion. It demands that one go out of one's way for another. So many of us never want to leave our comfort zone. Love cannot be a clean and sterile procedure. We have to be willing to get down and dirty. Just as the Samaritan put the unfortunate man on his beast, we must be willing to "trade places" to see what it is like on the other side of the tracks.

One serious blotch on the very soul of our country is racism. It can never be hidden. Just about 150 years ago the issue of racism helped create a great divide in the country contributing to the outbreak of the Civil War. The abolition of slavery changed the law of the land, but it has taken years of attitudinal change in the heart of man to make some dent in the malaise of bigotry. Racial cooperation does not come through legislation and judicial decision, as important as these may be. True racial parity comes when extrinsic, consensual outlooks are intrinsically assimilated into personal commitments and vital principles.

As we look out across the country to the face of the American Church, we can readily see that by and large the Church is not yet colorblind. The beauty of our diversity has not yet been realized. Much work needs to be accomplished for this goal to be realized. We are still reproducing carbon copies of the previous generation. We need to begin to think outside of the box. New power like that unleashed in atomic weaponry will surge forth when the creativity of our collective diversity is uncovered. Satan would like nothing better than to continue to blind our eyes so as to hide our light under a bushel basket. May our collective conscience in the Holy Spirit remove the blinders over our dimly lit eyesight.

Equal

In the Book of Acts, Peter's spiritual vision is found wanting and dim. God uses a trance to break Peter out of his narrow-minded views concerning the Gentile people.

Peter went up on the housetop about the sixth hour to pray. And he became hungry and was desiring to eat; but while they were making preparations, he fell into a trance; and he beheld the sky open up, and a certain object like a great sheet coming down, lowered by four corners to the ground, and there were in it all kinds of four-footed animals and crawling creatures of the earth and birds of the air. And a voice came to him, "Arise, Peter, kill and eat!" But Peter said, "By no means,

*Lord, for I have never eaten anything unholy and unclean."
And again a voice came a second time, "What God has
cleansed, no longer consider unholy" (Acts 10:9-15 NASB,
author emphasis added).*

The Mosaic Law prohibited eating certain unclean animals. Peter's insight filled his eyesight as God opened him up to an understanding about Gentiles. The case of Cornelius (see Acts 10:17) was revelation to Peter. It fueled and propelled the spread of the gospel to all nations with the force of a nuclear weapon. Could this newfound faith in Jesus be meant for people who were not Jewish? Could an "unclean," uncircumcised pagan be as viable a candidate for Christianity as the devout Jew? How could a heathen be considered equal to a religious Jew of the synagogue? These must have been questions running through the mind of Peter and the other apostles of the Lord.

Finally, God in His glory transforms Peter's insight into foresight giving him the long-range plan for a church without racist walls. And he said to them, *"You yourselves know how unlawful it is for a man who is a Jew to associate with a foreigner or to visit him; yet God has shown me that I should not call any man unholy or unclean"* (Acts 10:28 NASB). Peter then goes to the house of the Gentile Cornelius practicing what he just preached. He profoundly announces for the entire world to hear that the gospel is for all humankind. *"I most certainly understand now that God is not one to show partiality"* (Acts 10:34 NASB). God is no respecter of person; He is an inclusive God.

This year in a national news broadcast, a story ran of a homeless African-American man in Philadelphia who went to a high perch on a bridge over the Schuylkill River ready to jump off and take his life. One could easily see the anguish of the man as he from time to time pounded his fragile head against the steel beam braces of the bridge. Dozens of police, firefighters, and pedestrians stood around doing seemingly nothing as the man held on to the bridge. A boat rescue depot stood not more than one mile up the river, but no one ever came. No one seemed to approach the man to talk him down. No one climbed up to even try to dissuade his apparent intent.

I could not understand the puzzling scenario. The troubled man then took out his wallet, which likely contained his ID, and threw it to the police. I thought to myself, if ever he was trying to give a message that he was serious, it was then. Some more time passed. No action was taken by anyone. People simply milled around waiting and talking. Finally, the homeless man let go after about 20 minutes and plunged into the river some 50 feet below. It turned out that he couldn't swim, so he drowned.

I was deeply affected by this story. It was as if society was saying the homeless, African-American man didn't really matter. He had no family, no money, no status, and no power. His life was therefore inconsequential. God showed me that that man was Jesus Himself. I was reminded of the words of Jesus:

Then these righteous ones will reply, "Lord, when did we ever see You hungry and feed You? Or thirty and give You something to drink? Or a stranger and show You hospitality? Or naked and give You clothing? When did we ever see You sick or in prison, and visit You? And the King will tell them, "I assure you, when you did it to one of the least of these my brothers and sisters, you were doing it to Me!" (Matthew 25:37-40 NLT).

Jesus was moved by compassion for the lost, dying world. He went to a town called Nain. A widow, whose only son had just died, met Him. The word of God says, *"When the Lord saw her, His heart went out to her and He said, 'Don't cry'"* (Luke 7:13). When Jesus heard about his friend Lazarus dying, the word of God says, *"Jesus wept"* (John 11:35). Pain and suffering move the hand of God. *"For the Lord comforts His people and will have compassion on His afflicted ones"* (Isa. 49:13b). There was nothing "cold" about Jesus. Just as He was fully divine, He was fully human. The full gamut of emotion moved through His body. He wasn't like some New Age guru, detached, motionless, and unaffected by the things going on around Him. He felt for the crowds because they were like sheep without a shepherd.

Ruth

In the Book of Ruth, Naomi is forced to leave her homeland in Bethlehem (House of Bread) because of the outbreak of famine. Some ten years later in Moab, her husband and two sons die, leaving Naomi with two daugh-ters-in-law. Evil things happen to us when we find our-selves wandering into foreign lands. We are unprotected without the bread of His presence. Naomi had heard a "rumor" that there was a harvest of bread back in Bethlehem. One of the daughters-in-law by the name of Ruth decided to stay by the side of Naomi. Ruth learned a great deal from watching her mentor, and though she had no birthright into God's people by blood, she demon-strated her allegiance to Naomi. Because of her loyalty she came to be included as one of God's own as she labored in a new land of Judah. Ruth asks permission to glean in the fields, and it is here that Ruth meets her lover, Boaz.

God tells Moses to *"put the bread of the Presence on this table to be before Me at all times"* (Exod. 25:30). There is life in the Bread of His Presence; there is death outside the Bread of His Presence. A young Moabite named Ruth came to be favored by the Lord in the presence of bread. Boaz, who represents the God figure, seeks out the hand of Ruth in marriage. Boaz was the father of Obed, who was the father of Jesse, who was the father of David, the King of Israel. Ruth enters a royal heritage and inheritance though she had no standing from the world's point of view. In Ruth 3:8 Ruth is found lying at the feet of Boaz on the threshing floor where the wheat is uncovered from the shaft. An uncovering occurs wherever there is true love and regard for each other.

There is no mistaking who we are as we are uncovered before each other. There is no pretense or deceit in true love. Just as on the threshing floor, the uncovering of the shaft exposes the chaff and the wheat together. So too, before our Lord Jesus, we are exposed for what we are, and for better or for worse, we are still loved!

In our church gatherings and homes today we meet to "break the Bread of His Presence." The Lord wants us to do this in memory of Him. He longs to be remembered for His gracious act of selfless and pure love. He says, *"I have eagerly desired to eat this Passover with you"* (Luke 22:15). The bread is taken, blessed, and broken. It is then given and shared. Jesus says, "Do this in memory of Me" not only to be remembered, but also to be chosen, blessed, and broken bread for others. Our ultimate mandate is that we be given away and shared as consecrated, holy bread.

CHAPTER EIGHT

INTERCESSORS (THE GOLDEN ALTAR OF INCENSE)

The Golden Altar burning incense represents the high plane of worship one comes to before going beyond into the presence of God. Worship at this altar is worship of God. The priest makes prayer and intercession at the Altar as he offers the incense to the Lord. Before the priest could come before the Altar of Incense, he had to (1) offer sacrifice for sin with the shedding of blood at the Brazen Altar, and (2) wash off defilement and be cleansed with water at the Brazen Laver. This is consistent with what is found written in the Scriptures, *"Let us draw near with a sincere heart in full assurance of faith, having our hearts sprinkled clean from an evil conscience, and our bodies washed with pure water"* (Heb. 10:22 NASB). The teaching implied is quite clear, namely, for our prayers to be answered by God, we must be in proper relationship with God.

The fire on the Altar is *"to be kept burning continually; it is not to go out"* (Lev. 6:13). The fire itself came only from

127

the coals of the Brazen Altar. It was the same fire because only the fires of a sin offering secure our access to God. This fire was used to consume the incense. The Golden Altar appears to be a replication of the divine order of worship in Heaven. The Book of Revelation states,

Another angel, who had a golden censer, came and stood at the altar. He was given much incense to offer, with the prayers of all the saints, on the golden altar before the throne. The smoke of the incense, together with the prayers of the saints, went up before God from the angel's hand (Revelation 8:3-4).

The fact that the nostrils of God receive the incense speaks about how very pleasing the scent of prayer is to Him. But the passage of Scripture continues, *"And the angel took the censor; and filled it with fire from the altar and threw it to the earth; and there came peals of thunder and sounds of flashes of lightening and an earthquake"* (Rev. 8:5). This is an illustration of a miracle! Following our prayer, God directs the angelic, incense bearer to hurl our prayers now mixed with the fires of Heaven back down upon the earth. The Heavenly fires, with sounds of thunder and flashes of lightening, pierce the darkness on the earth. Prayer releases the light of God to penetrate the darkness. Darkness cannot co-exist with the light. For light overshadows darkness. *"The light shines through the darkness, and the darkness can never extinguish it"* (John 1:5 NLT). Prayer and the intercession of the saints release the power of God in the earth. This is an awesome revelation!

Intercession

In the Book of Exodus, Pharaoh instructed the Hebrew midwives:

"When you help the Hebrew women in childbirth, and observe them on the delivery stool, if it is a boy, kill him; but if it is a girl, let her live." The midwives, however feared God and did not do what the king of Egypt had told them to do; they let the boys live (Exodus 1:16-17).

It was the role of the midwife to act as a "*go between*" the mother and the child to be born. A midwife is an intercessor, a "go between" bringing to birth the child of promise. Moses came forth as the child of the promise to deliver the people of Israel. He was born as a direct result of the faithfulness of the midwives to God. They decided it was better to obey God and fear Him than to obey Pharaoh and fear him. Intercession brings forth the child of promise. The intercessor acts like a midwife struggling to bring the birth into reality. The prayers go up before the Holy One, and the answer breaks forth into reality.

This is what our great High Priest does for us even now. The presence of the Lamb before the Ancient of Days in Heaven is a continual and lasting testament to His Intercession on behalf of all humankind. *"But Jesus remains a priest forever; His priesthood will never end. Therefore, He is able, once and forever, to save everyone who comes to God through Him. He lives forever to plea with God on their behalf"* (Heb. 7:24-25 NLT).

When praying prayers of intercession, several dramatic changes take place:

a. Intercession changes the mind of God.

In the Book of Exodus, Moses went up Mount Sinai to receive the Ten Commandments from God. The people of Israel are found worshiping the golden calf. God is angry at the Israelites because of their sin of idolatry. Yet, Moses pleads his case with God on behalf of the people of Israel. Listen to how he prays to God:

Then the Lord God said to Moses, "Go down, because your people, whom you brought up out of Egypt, have become corrupt. They have been quick to turn away from what I commanded them and have made an idol cast in the shape of a calf." God continues, "I have seen these people, and they are a stiff-necked people. Now leave Me alone so that My anger may burn against them and that I may destroy them."

But Moses sought the favor of the Lord his God. "O Lord," he said, "why should Your anger burn against Your people, whom You brought out of Egypt with great power and a mighty hand? Why should the Egyptians say, 'it was with evil intent that He brought them out, to kill them in the mountains and to wipe them from the face of the earth?' Turn from Your fierce anger; relent and do not bring disaster on Your people. Remember Your servants Abraham, Isaac, and Israel, to whom You swore Yourself: "I will make your descendents as numerous as the stars in the sky and I will give your descendents all this land I promised them and I will be their inheritance forever." Then the Lord relented and did not bring on His people the disaster He had threatened" (Exodus 32:7-14, author emphasis added).

The sin of idolatry made the people of Israel liable to the judgment of God. They could not presume on His grace and forgiveness. There is always judgment for sin. There are always consequences for our wrongdoing. Notice how God casts the people off to Moses by calling them "Your" people not My people. Moses pleads his case to the Lord and argues before God. He intercedes on behalf of the Israelites in spite of their corrupt sin. He reminds God of His promises, which He made to the people. He calls the people "Your" people to God. He appeals to God's mercy, and God relents on His anger. Intercession releases the mercy of God.

The prelude to any kind of personal or corporate change must begin with repentance. Because of our personal sin and corporate sin as a nation, a people, and as a world, there is stark need to fall to our knees pleading the mercies of our God. The biblical principle of sowing and reaping is so evident and telling about what has transpired. A life is fruitful or fruitless based on the principle of sowing and reaping. In the Book of Deuteronomy one sees God teach blessings for obedience and curses for disobedience.

If you fully obey the Lord your God and carefully follow all His commands I give you this day, the Lord your God will set you high above all the nations on earth. All these blessings will come upon you and accompany you if you obey the Lord your God: You will be blessed in the city and blessed in the country. The fruit of your womb will be blessed, and the crops of your land and the young of your livestock...You will be blessed when you come in and when you go out. The Lord will grant that the enemies who rise up against you will be defeated before you...The Lord will open the Heavens, the storehouse of His bounty, to send rain on your land in season and to bless all the works of your hands. You will lend to many nations but will borrow from none. The Lord will make you the head, not the tail (Deuteronomy 28:1-7a,12-13).

However, curses will follow if one does not obey the commands of the Lord. *"The sky over your head will be bronze, the ground beneath you iron"* (Deut. 28:23). In other words, the prayers offered by the disobedient will not be answered. These prayers will bounce off the sky of bronze.

There is not an open heaven here. The reason these intercessory prayers aren't answered may be due to personal sin or it may be due to the sins of the fathers. Repentance brings us to a place of humility before God as we ask for His forgiveness for personal, generational, and corporate sin. God instructs us:

If My people, who are called by My name, will humble themselves and pray and seek My face and turn from their wicked ways, then will I hear from Heaven and will forgive their sin and heal their land" (2 Chronicles 7:14).

Our prayer should be:

God our Father, we humbly come before You to say we have sinned against You. We have sinned against Your holy precepts and have disobeyed Your perfect laws. Our pride and selfishness has risen up against You. We have fallen far short of Your glory and have dishonored You. Forgive us of our rebellious ways, O Lord. We have not loved You with all our heart, soul, and strength. We have wandered far from Your path of righteousness. Our sin has dimmed our vision. Remove from us our shortsightedness; blot out our offenses. Take us back in Your loving kindness. Spread Your mercy over us and our fathers who have sinned against You, we pray. Without You, Father, our life is meaningless. Do not continue to hide Your face from us. We know we are unworthy of Your goodness, yet, in Your great compassion find it in Your heart to take us back as Your own. We offer this prayer to You in the name of Your son, Jesus Who died to make us Your own. Amen.

If serious prayer warriors direct prayer to remove the brass heavens over their heads, and the bronze clay under their feet, God will remove spiritual dominion that continues to keep people in bondage.

b. Intercession dispels the darkness.

It takes powerful and persistent prayer to get a breakthrough. That is why the word of God is full of narratives teaching the importance of persistent prayer. One might ask, "Why doesn't God simply give in to me and my prayer request?" The answer to this question lies in the reality that the Heavens above can be covered with evil forces of darkness hindering the answer to our prayer. There is likely a shield or veil of darkness covering us. The reason has nothing to do with God not wanting to give us something that is good for our lives.

The word says, *"On this mountain the Lord Almighty will destroy the shroud (veil) that enfolds all peoples, the sheet that covers all nations; He will swallow up death forever"* (Isa. 25:7-8a). Sin, sickness, and death are the enemies of God. The devil comes to rob, kill and destroy. Believers need to be aware of the demonic forces of darkness in the heavens shrouding the quality of their life.

Intercession shoots arrows into the darkness above, destroying the works of the devil. The prophet Elisha commanded the king of Israel, *"'take the bow in your hands, and open the east window and shoot! The Lord's arrow of victory over Aram! You will completely destroy the Armeans at Aphek'"* (see 2 Kings 13:16-17). Persistence in striking the ground with the arrows would have clinched decisive victory over Aram. The king only struck the ground three times when he needed to strike it five or six times.

Intercession causes a stir in Heaven. When Heaven is stirred, angels are stirred in your behalf. Ministering angels are dispatched in your behalf. God Himself on the throne begins to stir at the sound of intercession.

Intercession puts God on His feet. Every time you see God spoken about in the Bible He is seated on the throne. The only time one sees God standing is to fight. God never fights sitting down. He stands and shows forth His great judgment. *"Let God arise, let His enemies be scattered"* (Ps. 68:1 NASB). God is referred to as a "man of war" in the word of the Lord rather than a "God of war." Both Moses and Isaiah reference God as a "man of war" (see Exod. 15:3; Isa. 42:13). This is so because when God is involved in a battle, He does it through men. Moses was sent to war against Pharaoh; Elijah was sent to war against the prophets of Baal; Jesus came as a man to destroy the works of the devil.

Victory in the land comes with obedience to God and intercessory prayer. Argentina is a country in South America that has experienced the revival fires due to obedience and intercessory prayer. On my recent trip there this past fall, Carlos Annacondia's interpreter told me that about 70 percent of the people in the country are born-again believers. This does not yet include the capital city of Buenos Aires, which still needs to be won for the Lord. How did such a revival occur in Argentina? Is it all due to powerful evangelists like Carlos Annacondia? Some history is in order to answer this question.

In the 1950s Edward Miller worked with about 50 Argentine Bible students. Classes were suspended because the nation was upon the hearts of the students and Edward Miller. They cried out to God for revival in the land. They sought God to release His Holy Spirit upon the nation. God honored their intercessory prayer with a divine visitation.

The divine encounter came after hours and days of weeping and crying out to God for mercy. The dry wasteland needed to be watered. In those days the government of Juan Peron ruled. There was only a handful of Spirit-filled believers. But that small seed offering blossomed into the great explosion of belief that they have today. On the fiftieth day of prayer and weeping, Dr. Miller heard a word of prophecy: "Weep no more, for the Lion of the tribe of Judah has prevailed over the prince of Argentina." Eighteen months following the prophecy, people began to pour into soccer stadiums by the hundred thousands. Intercession had pierced the darkness. Revival had been birthed out of travail and intercession.

c. Intercession kills the flesh.

Prayer breaks the bondage of our natural appetites. Our flesh needs to die to its desires and cravings. One cannot train the flesh or change the flesh. It must be killed. Jesus reminds us, *"If anyone would come after Me, he must deny himself, take up his cross and follow Me"* (Matt. 16:24 NASB). As one dies to self, one grows in His Spirit. It is the Holy Spirit who draws and quickens to pray. Just as John the Baptist learned, one learns to decrease that He might increase. No flesh can stand in the presence of God.

In 1997, in Springfield, Illinois a pastor, Donna Auerbach, was driving her car on her way to a revival meeting I was holding in Peoria. Along the highway, she noticed a young hitchhiker. Out of character for her, she stopped to give him a ride. It happened that the young man was on the FBI runaway list since he was 14 years old. He was currently 22. He had no home, no friends, and no place to go.

The pastor decided to bring Mike to the revival meeting. Mike agreed while in her car that it was time to get his life straightened out with God. He was beaten as a child by his father, lived a life on drugs and alcohol, and had turned his life toward satanism. At ministry time the pastor brought Mike forward for prayer. He had many thick silver chains around his neck. He was dressed in all black with heavy silver chains around his waist. His body was tattooed with skull and crossbones, a pentagram, and the words *"death is life."* The knuckles on his left hand spelled out the word *pain.*

I told him the words and insignias on his body were lies. I told him that the devil had lied to him. I told him Jesus wanted him as His friend, and that only Jesus could set him free from the bondage. Mike indicated that he wanted Jesus, so I cast out all demons from his body. He fell to the floor and writhed like a snake until in a matter of a few minutes he was set free. He then invited Jesus into his heart, and cried like a child for the love of God he had never known before. That night the Lover of his soul and the Father to this son met in an emotional embrace.

Let me update the story of this young man. The young man's appetite is now whetted and hungry for the Lord. He went on to get his GED, works for the local church, and is enrolled in Bible school to be a minister of the gospel to those in the bondage of hell. Mike Evans has reunited with his mother in Louisiana who is a believer. She never ceased praying and interceding for her son. For all those years the woman placed Scripture quotes on the FBI Internet reports concerning her son. Prayer works! Let us never give up.

Adoration

Most of the appointments of the Tabernacle are spoken of in terms of things to come in the Messiah. But the Lord God tells Moses to make sure this fragrant incense is burning on the Altar always.

And Aaron shall burn fragrant incense on it; he shall burn it every morning when he trims the lamps. And when Aaron trims the lamps at twilight, he shall burn incense. There shall be perpetual incense before the Lord throughout your generations (Exodus 30:7-8 NASB, author emphasis added).

Here one sees a ministry, which extends from eternity to eternity. It is the picture of pure adoration given to God. These prayers ask nothing for themselves; they only direct praise and worship to Him. The prayer of adoration is the highest order of prayer. Its purpose is to extol the beauty of the Lord God Most High. This type of intercession is not for the needs of the people. Here one ministers only unto God. The pure, unadulterated prayer of adoration is recorded in the Book of Revelation.

And [the four living creatures and the twenty-four elders] sang a new song: "You are worthy to take the scroll and to open its seals, because You were slain, and with Your blood You purchased men for God from every tribe and language and people and nation. You have made them to be a kingdom and priests to serve our God, and they will reign on the earth." Then I looked and heard the voice of many angels, numbering thousands upon thousands, and ten thousand times ten thousand. They encircled the throne and the living creatures and the elders. In a loud voice they sang: "Worthy is the Lamb, who was slain, to receive power and wealth and wisdom and strength and honor and glory and praise!" Then I heard every creature in heaven and on earth and under the earth and on the sea, and all that is in them, singing: "To Him who sits on the throne and unto the Lamb be praise and honor and glory and power, forever and ever" (Revelation 5:9-13).

Incense

The incense offered on the Altar of Incense was a sweet spice of aromatic dried resins that were made for perfume. Four resins are listed in Exodus 30:34-35 for incense. *"Then the Lord said to Moses, 'take fragrant spices-stacte, onycha, galbanum, and pure frankincense, all in equal amounts, and make a fragrant blend of incense, the work of a perfumer.'"*

Stacte is the first resin used in the composite called incense. This sweet spice comes from a tree that grows in Israel and Syria. The resin oozed out of the tree freely. The spiritual implication here is that our praise must come out of us freely. Praise of the Lord becomes something one wants to freely offer back to the Lord. It oozes out of us like the gum stacte.

Onycha is a finely ground powder from a shellfish. This particular shellfish is found in the Red Sea even to this day. In order to catch the fish, one must dive down to 400-600 meters deep. This implies that a relationship with God requires that one go deep with Him. This cannot be a superficial relationship. We must be willing to go deep for the deeper things of God. The shells, which were retrieved from the deep, were ground into fine powder and burned as incense to produce a sweet fragrance.

Galbanum is a gum from the Merle tree. The limbs of this tree split allowing the resin to come forth. Splitting is about breaking open. It gives forth its fine resin only after breaking open. Splitting and breaking speak of pain. It is out of our pain that the fragrance of God comes forth. In the New Testament the mother of Zebedee's sons come to Jesus asking Him for special places next to Him in His kingdom one day. Jesus asked them, *"Can you drink the cup I am going to drink?"* (Matt. 20:22). Jesus is asking if anyone who aspires to a place of position in the Kingdom can drink the cup of suffering it takes to secure such positions. He was referring specifically to the kind of death He would endure for our eternal life.

Frankincense comes from a tree that also splits. The resin seeps out only during the hours of the early watch. This would mean about four in the morning. Another word for seeping is "weeping." Intercessors are called to weep before the Lord in the early watch of the morning.

God then tells Moses to take salt to temper the spices. It is then to be ground into powder. Pharmaceutical companies use all four of these resins for healing and medicinal purposes. God shows Moses how to blend the resins like an apothecary. The grinding into powder represents the holiness pleasing to the Lord. God is demonstrating through these resins that true prayer flows out of the issues of the heart. The heart is prepared through the trials and suffering it faces in a lifetime. To learn the meaning of praying out of the issues of the heart means one can begin to enter into the very presence of the Lord.

Revisiting the Holy Place

We have examined the Holy Place as a place where one finds (a) the Golden Lampstand, (b) the Altar of Showbread, and (c) the Golden Altar of Incense. As one stops at each station, I cannot help realizing that the quality of the oil, the bread, and the incense is produced only after a carefully followed process.

The oil comes forth only after laborious pressing of the olive; the bread is produced only after thrashing and kneading the grain of wheat; and the incense only results from much crushing and grinding. We can only conclude that the Holy Place makes holy through crushing and pain. It is God's surgery room where He cuts out the flesh, which separates us from Him. It is a place of travail and at times a valley of tears. The rewards of being "refined in the fire" are dramatic. True change to our character emerges when we spend time in the Holy Place. Time before the Lampstand yields the gifts and fruits of the Holy Spirit; time with the Showbread brings reconciliation, unity and fellowship; and time with the censor of incense brings forth an unselfish spirit of prayer and thanksgiving.

None of us likes suffering. But God uses suffering as the way to purification and holiness. God uses the trials in our life to bring forth His character in us. The Letter of James says:

Consider it pure joy, my brothers, whenever you face trials of many kinds, because you know that the testing of your faith develops perseverance. Perseverance must finish its work so that you may be mature and complete, not lacking anything (James 1:2-4).

And again Paul speaks to us out of the Book of Romans: *"We also rejoice in our sufferings, because we know that suffering produces perseverance; perseverance, character; and character hope"* (Rom.5:3-4). Finally, Peter tells us:

Do not be surprised at the painful trial you are suffering, as though something strange was happening to you. But rejoice that you participate in the sufferings of Christ, so that you may be overjoyed when His glory is revealed (1 Peter 4:12-13).

Some Christians live with the fallacy that because they are born again and Spirit filled, no problems should come their way. God's word promises that problems and sufferings will come our way, but He also promises that we will be more than a conqueror. Each one of these trials is indicative of our growth in the Lord. Each one of these increasingly demanding trials is an opportunity for our flesh to die and our dependency on God to soar. God must make the container able to carry the grace of His presence. God builds the character to hold the grace.

In the story of Elijah the prophet, Elisha is his apprentice. In the Second Book of Kings, Elijah encouraged Elisha to stay behind on a journey that would take the prophet to Bethel, then Jericho, and finally, across the Jordan. The student of prophecy protested to his elder. He said as long as he lived, he would be faithful in not leaving him. *"As surely as the Lord lives and as you live, I will not leave you"* (2 Kings 2:2b). God rewards the diligent that pursue after Him. Elijah's journey to the three mentioned locations represents Elisha's willingness to follow the man of God for the fullness of the spiritual journey.

The three vignettes symbolize three spiritual weigh stations. Bethel represents the place where one comes to know God. *Bethel* means "house of God." It is noted as the place where God reveals Himself to Jacob. Moving on through life one comes to Jericho. It is a place that has seen a great deal of warfare and combat. It is the place that Joshua marched around seven times, and on the last time blew the trumpet for God. The sound caused the walls to come tumbling down. Finally, the Jordan River marks the crossing over into the Promised Land. Here is the place of deliverance and blessing. Because of the faithfulness of Elisha he is rewarded with a double portion of the spirit of his father Elijah. Character must be developed on the journey in order to carry the presence of the Lord's power.

People come forward in the prayer lines at miracle services. Many ask their pastors to pray for them to receive the gifts. Pastors want them to be sure they are willing to die to their flesh to carry the gift. The spiritual journey must be walked from Bethel to Jericho to the Jordan. The character necessary to carry the gifting must be developed by trial and fire. We must be willing to go into the Holy Place and allow God to perform His spiritual surgery. Here we die that He might be born anew.

PART THREE
STEPPING INTO PASSION

CHAPTER NINE

HIS PRESENCE (THE ARK OF THE COVENANT)

The Veil

If we were to gaze at the sweet incense rising up as smoke from the Altar, the imposing sight of the veil before us would be captivating. The veil was a thin, ornamental curtain that divided the Holy Place from the Most Holy Place. In that sense it functioned like no other curtain because it hung as a great line of demarcation between where God dwelt and where man could go. Man was separated from God because of his sin. There would be no crossing the line until sin had been removed. Man had no access into the presence of God. The glory of God was withheld from man.

Only the high priest could venture beyond the veil on the Day of Atonement. History records the high priest feared for his life going into the Most Holy Place. A long rope was tied to his ankle in the event he needed to be pulled from God's presence if he failed to come out from the overwhelming presence of God. What may have happened to the high priest before the Lord Most High was that he was slain in the Spirit as he stepped behind the veil.

The colorful veil was embroidered with images of cherubim. The linen tapestry had twisted threads of blue, purple, and scarlet woven through it. The two cherubim stretched forth the shadow of their wings before the ministering priest. It was as if the angels gestured with their wings to "keep out." The subsequent veil in the Second Temple had no figures on it.

The Tabernacle veil hid away from man the glory of God Almighty. The veil gives one the same imagery that was brought to earth in the incarnate Word. *"The Word became flesh and dwelt among us. We have seen His glory, the glory of the one and only Son, who came from the Father, full of grace and truth"* (John 1:14). Like the veil, which hid away the glory of the Lord Most High, Jesus in His flesh hid away the glory of the Lord Most High.

Just as one needed to look beyond the veil to capture a glimpse of God, one needed to look beyond the flesh of Jesus to behold His glory. A limited, earth-bound mind might only see a man as it looked at Jesus of Nazareth. An empirical mind-set would only see a beautiful tapestry in the veil of the Tabernacle. The empirical mind would say, "Jesus was a revolutionary teacher of the Law who happened to make eccentric claims. He may have had delusional features that He struggled with in His adult life. He was idealistic and misguided, but all in all made some contribution to the reformation of religion."

This interpretation is strictly biased by a limited, near-sighted vision. To step into the realm of faith takes one beyond the "veil" of the curtain and beyond the "veil" of the humanity of Jesus. It gives us eyes by which we can see transcendence in the face of the natural, and the extraordinary in the face of the ordinary.

Luke strongly suggests that Jesus defined and identified His life and calling when He unrolled the scroll of the sacred Scripture in His hometown of Nazareth and read:

The Spirit of the Lord is upon Me, because He has anointed Me to preach good news to the poor. He has sent me to proclaim freedom for the prisoners and recovery of sight for the blind, to release the oppressed, to proclaim the year of the Lord's favor (Luke 4:18-19).

Spiritual Myopia

Jesus is claiming to be the fulfillment of this prophecy when He simply says, *"Today this scripture is fulfilled in your hearing"* (Luke 4:21). Jesus claims to be the Messiah before His townspeople. They know Jesus to be the son of Joseph. How could He claim to be extraordinary? The natural eye is so limited in what it sees. It cannot see the true origin of the Son of God. The ear of the people could only hear blasphemy in His words. They could not hear the celestial roar and applause for Jesus at that moment by the throngs of Heaven. The public proclamation became an outcry. Rejection came to be their only recourse, in order to set in stone their traditional way of thinking.

Let one not think that rejection of the divinity of Jesus is limited to the Jewish world. Rejection of Jesus stands as a potential response to everyone with near-sightedness. The mystery of the veil of the Tabernacle is blessed to those with eyes to see. The knowledge of the secrets of the Kingdom of God is given to them that see. C.M. Spurgeon writes in his work *The Early Years*, (1834-1859) about the form of God's coming in revival:

Observe how sovereign the operations of God are… He may in one area work revival, and persons may be stricken down, and made to cry aloud, but in another place there may be crowds and yet all may be still and quiet as though no deep excitement existed at all. He can bless as He will and He will bless as He wills. Let us not dictate to God. Many a blessing has been lost by Christians not believing it to be a blessing because it did not come in the particular shape which they had conceived to be proper and right.[xiv]

Paul reminds us that Christ Jesus, *"Who, being in very nature God, did not consider equality with God something to be grasped, but made Himself nothing, taking the very nature of a servant, being made in human likeness"* (Phil. 2:6-7).

Jesus, fully God, chose to empty Himself by assuming the very nature of humanity with all its limitations. He came in the likeness of the flesh. He was tempted like we are; He offered prayer and supplication with loud cries and groaning. He learned obedience even to His death on the cross. Through the rent veil of His body, His life was yielded and laid down freely as a gift for purchase. It took the death of God Himself to reconcile all creation to God. The renting of the veil opened up God's glory for us.

It is interesting that at the time of the death of Jesus at 3:00 PM on Good Friday afternoon on Mount Calvary, the Temple's thick veil was rent asunder. The torn veil of Jesus tore away that which separated man from God in the Holy Temple. Andrew Murray writes in his *The Holiest of All* (Whitaker House, 1996):

The way into the Holiest (Most Holy Place) is the way of the rent veil, the way of sacrifice and death. There is no way for our putting away sin from us but the way of Jesus; whoever accepts His finished work accepts what constitutes its Spirit and power; it is for every man as for the Master-to put away sin by the sacrifice of self. Christ's death was something entirely and essentially new, and so also His resurrection life; a life out of death, such as never had been known before. This new death and new life constitute the new and living way, the new way of living in which we draw near to God.[xv]

The new way is the way of death to self. Jesus said it in terms of an analogy.

I tell you the truth, unless a kernel of wheat falls to the ground and dies, it remains only a single seed. But if it dies, it produces many seeds. The man who loves his life will lose it, while the man who hates his life in this world will keep it for eternal life (John 12:24-25).

Someone once said, "God can only use dead men." The way of death is the way to life. We must die to the flesh and its fallen nature of sin in order to be transformed in the power of His resurrection. The sacrifice of Jesus, our High Priest, is not a quid pro quo, but a gratuitous act of pure mercy from God. It is His proof and evidence of His love for us all. The sacrifice of Jesus is the *"sine qua non,"* for without it there is no redemption for us.

Pure Benevolence

The French Easter liturgy records, *"L'amour de Dieu est folie"* or "the love of God is foolishness." The sacrifice of our God lends one to rethink all images of justice and fair play. To celebrate this lavish kind of grace speaks to the essence and kernel of the Book of Hebrews. Jesus magnanimously cancels our rightful debt and recreates our human nature into His nature and likeness. It is like the butterfly unfolding and transforming before our very eyes.

His act of benevolence renders our transformation possible. None of this profuse gifting depended on anything from us. Our part is simply to receive it. His act is entirely given to all humankind in an unconditional, unrequited, and unmerited fashion. Brennan Manning writes in his poignant book *Lion and Lamb* (Chosen Books, 1986) about the relentless tenderness of Jesus. This wonderful man burns with a passion for Jesus, and a love for the common man rarely seen. Brennan says, "the gospel of Jesus Christ is the love story of God with us. Forgiveness is granted (the sinner); it need only be accepted. This is real amnesty—gratis."xvi

In 1982, as a Roman Catholic priest, I realized what Martin Luther some centuries ago came to realize, namely, that Jesus Christ came to fulfill the need for a sacrificial priesthood. As a Catholic priest I was ordained to act as intermediary between God and my people. I offered Mass for the sins of the people. I heard confession and absolved sin. I realized what Jesus did on Calvary sufficed. Sin was atoned for through His sacrifice once for all. There was no need for any other sacrifice. He alone is our High Priest.

Jesus opened a way for "the priesthood for all believers." As one comes to Him, one becomes *a chosen people, a royal priesthood, a holy nation, a people belonging to God"* (1 Pet. 2:9). I was called to be a minister, but only Jesus was called to be our priest. The Spirit of God was faithful to lead me in the ways of the truth!

However, the following months were difficult. I had left the priesthood. A great price was paid because now I had no job, and for that matter, no home. I had given 17 years of my life toward the priesthood. It was all I knew, yet God honors obedience.

I was to do a conference during the summer of 1983 with healing evangelist R.W. Shambock in Indianapolis. This man is a spiritual father to many young healing evangelists. Likewise, I had an invitation to Trinity Broadcasting Network in California. TBN was looking for someone with a true gift of healing. The television network heard about my ministry and wanted to use televised healing services to reach the nation. I declined both of these invitations and left the ministry. I believe God had a great plan in mind that I decided not to follow.

I retreated back into my head, which is a comfortable place for many of us to live. In making my mind my confidant, I made the inevitable mistake of leaving my heart. I went back to the university, rather than trusting the path that God had planned for me. By taking our life into our own hands, we take it out of God's hands.

Think of King Uzziah of Judah. God blessed this young king with a wonderful, creative mind. He invented military offensive and defensive weaponry for Jerusalem, weaponry that was used hundreds of years into the future by the Roman Empire.

The word of God says, *"His fame spread far and wide, for he was greatly helped, until he became powerful"* (2 Chron. 26:15). Strength in the flesh leads to pride. Paul gloried in his weakness because it was then that he was strong. Pride led to the downfall of Uzziah. He wanted to burn incense in the Temple of the Lord when this was the role of the priest. Uzziah was called to be king, not priest. When one walks out of their known calling one walks in sin. The priests protested against the king in vain. He raged at the priests before the Altar of Incense, and leprosy broke out on the king's forehead. Uzziah led the rest of his life in isolation and despair. Uzziah was a man who started out right, but ended up wrong. He left the call of God on his life to do something else.

I left the call of God to do something else. I leaned upon my own understanding. The journey away from the ministry represented a journey away from God. I found myself worshiping at the door of the intellect.

Please don't misunderstand me. To go back to the university for higher education was not wrong or evil. It can be stimulating and creative. It is only wrong for one who steps out of one's call. I support higher education, especially for church leadership. Intelligence does not have to be sacrificed as a casualty of church life. Christians need to be clear on what they believe and be in a position to articulate such beliefs when questioned. I believe in excellence with our minds, but I believe our minds need to be subordinated to the wisdom of Almighty God. God reminds us, *"Trust in the Lord with all your heart and lean not upon your own understanding. In all your ways acknowledge Him, and He will make your paths straight"* (Prov. 3:5-6).

In pursing doctoral level psychology, I found myself quickly on a slippery slope. I convinced myself that I was strong enough to hold onto my faith in an arena that gave no place for the Lord. God carefully teaches us that we cannot mix the things above with the things below. He says, *"Be careful not to make a treaty with those who live in the land where you are going, or they will snare you. Break down their altars, smash their sacred stones, and cut down their Asherah poles"* (Exod. 34:12-13).

Passing through the veil requires that we keep our focus on Him. Like Peter walking on the water, we must keep our eyes focused on Him. When we take our eyes off God, we are bound to fall and lose sight of our true pursuit. Beyond the veil there is only the Lord. There is no one else to trust. Others can no longer advise you how to walk. You are on your own.

The Ark of the Covenant

Beyond the curtain lies the Ark of the Covenant. In a most generic way, the Ark symbolizes God's central desire to "dwell among us." It is by far the most special piece of furniture in the Tabernacle. It is the first piece of furniture commanded by God to be made.

Have them make a chest of acacia wood—two and a half cubits long, a cubit and a half wide, and a cubit and a half high. Overlay it with pure gold, both inside and out, and make a gold molding around it. Cast four gold rings for it and fasten them to its four feet, with two rings on one side and two rings on the other. Then make poles of acacia wood and overlay them with gold. Insert the poles into the rings on the sides of the chest to carry it. The poles are to remain in the rings of this ark; they are not to be removed. Then put in the ark the Testimony, which I will give you (Exodus 25:10-16).

Here one can see the Ark typifying the humanity and divinity of our Lord. Just as wood and gold worked in concert to form the Ark of God's presence, Jesus' humanity and divinity combine to form a unique and beautiful tapestry of the God we can know and worship. The Ark is a clear symbol of Christ's nature. But what was God referring to when He said to put into the Ark "the Testimony" which He would give them? For this answer one needs to look into the Book of Hebrews:

> *This Ark contained the gold jar of manna, Aaron's rod that had budded, and the stone tablets of the covenant. Above the Ark were the cherubim of the Glory, overshadowing the place of atonement. But we cannot discuss these things in detail now (Hebrews 9:4b-5).*

More than anything else in the Tabernacle, the Ark evokes a sense of the majesty and awe of the Lord God. It lends one to ponder the transcendent power of God, His beauty and radiance, and His unparalleled command and sovereignty over all. The very word *"God"* means "He who needs no one else or nothing else in order to exist." God is self-sufficient and self-sustaining. This means He doesn't need us to believe in Him in order to be God. He is God whether we believe in Him or not.

Friedrich Nietzsche (1844-1900) influenced the Nazi movement during World War II with his "will to power" theme. During his lifetime Nietzsche pronounced God to be dead. He claimed the discoveries of Galileo, Copernicus, and Darwin proved the ineffectiveness and impotence of religion. When Nietzsche died in 1900, it is said that a public notice read, "'Nietzsche is dead'—signed God."

Such naturalistic beliefs are not new to God. He has dealt with these arguments throughout the history of humanity. Pundits like Bertrand Russell have argued against rational theses on the existence of God. Christian philosophers and scientists have crafted and developed sound arguments like the First Cause theory, the theory of Natural Law, the argument by Design, and the Laws of Morality for years. Pundits view Christian tenets as a crutch or needless dependencies. Some deny the very existence of Jesus Christ, while others see the Church as retarding the moral progress of man's soul.

I believe God leaves His fingerprints in each of the above arguments; however, knowledge of God can only be "known" by taking the step of faith into God. The Danish philosopher Soren Kierkegaard (1813-1855) understood it correctly when he said that in order for one to know God one had to take of "leap of faith."

Transcendent Yet Immanent

The belief that God is immanent as well as transcendent can be considered because God abides in His creation. While He lives in it, He is not limited by it. While He is present to creation, He is not the sum of its parts. Divine presence in creation does not presuppose pantheism. Things that are ultimately corruptible and finite cannot define God's glory. He is above all His works while immanent to them.

This is precisely why we can say God is everywhere. Whether we are aware of this truth or not, it does not alter the theological truth that God is omnipresent and omniscient. As we take the "leap of faith," we discover the reality of God and His immanent presence.

For since the creation of the world, God's invisible qualities, His eternal power and divine nature, have been clearly seen, being understood from what has been made, so that men are without excuse (Romans 1:20).

The leap into faith sets our feet on a journey directed toward relationship with God. The more we taste the goodness of the Lord, the more we seem to want to pursue Him. It is not simply enough to be "saved." We find out He is more precious than gold. We seek after His presence with abandon. We press in for more on our walk through the Tabernacle. The Ark of His presence is our lifeline. We must be in contact with Him. We can have it no other way. With David, we cry out for the Ark of His presence. Seeking after His presence becomes more important than eating and drinking. Being in His presence is life.

The Ark had a long history of leading the people of Israel through the desert wilderness as they went from Sinai to Kadesh-Barnea (see Num. 10:33). As the Ark of God led the way for the people, the people followed. Moses knew that if he were to lead the people through the desert to the land of promise, he had better follow the leading and prompting of the Lord God. Moses had learned the power in being obedient and the consequences of being disobedient to God. He was most careful in following all the directives of the Lord God regarding the making of the Tabernacle. When the work was complete, a cloud of the glory of God covered the Tabernacle.

Whenever the cloud would lift from above the Tabernacle, Moses would know God wanted them to strike camp, for it was time to move on in their journey. Whenever the cloud would settle over the Tabernacle, it indicated it was time to make camp. A cloud was over the Tabernacle by day, and a pillar of fire was in the cloud by night (see Exod. 40:3).

But what was this "cloud" that could be visibly seen over the Tabernacle? It was the presence of God. When Moses pleaded with the Lord for the Lord's presence to go with him and the people of Israel, this is what Moses was talking about.

Then Moses said to Him, "If Your Presence does not go with us, do not send us up from here. How will anyone know that You are pleased with me and with Your people unless You go with us?" (Exodus 33:15-16)

After pleading with the Lord to dwell among them in His presence, Moses continues on to express another important point. *"What else will distinguish me and Your people from all the other people on the face of the earth"* (Exod. 33:16). Moses is saying that unless God's presence remains with them, they will be no different from any other people on the earth. Think of this. It is the presence of God that makes the difference in the life of a believer. Recall Moses coming down the mountain of the Lord, and his face was radiant, because he had been speaking to the Lord in the in His presence. The friends of Moses were afraid to come near him because his face glowed with the glory of God.

The cloud of glory was the very presence of God. The very thing that distinguished the people of Israel from all other people was the presence of God. The radiance on the face of Moses was the presence of God. The presence of the Lord is sensible and tangible. It could be seen and detected over the Tabernacle and on the face of Moses. This manifested presence is different than the usual omnipresence of God. For in it God breaks into our dimension of existence in a sensible and tangible way. It becomes recognizable when He comes and when He goes. It is as if a person in the flesh walks into a room and one can see and perceive him. The same is true when the manifest presence of God appears. Like a cloud it moves in and moves out. It often lingers for hours or for days at a time. It comes in the midst of praise and worship. It drops down among the people to be absorbed. To be in its presence is to absorb its essence. Just as Moses displayed the presence of God's radiance, it can light us up in holiness, power, and grace.

Shekinah

The people of Israel referred to this type of presence of God as the Shekinah glory of God. Psalm 18 refers to the *Shekinah* as "the brightness of His Presence." It is the

Shekinah glory that settled on Mount Sinai and over the Mercy Seat of the Tabernacle. The Bible is saying that without the manifest presence of God things become ordinary. With the manifest presence of God things become extraordinary.

In 1996, I had the opportunity to preach and teach at Toronto Airport Christian Fellowship church for four days. It was there in January 1994 that the first signs of this tangible presence of God broke out since the charismatic renewal in the 1967 in America. Millions of people from all parts of the world came to experience the Lord's presence. This move of God has been criticized by some who haven't "entered in," but far more have been revitalized with the fire of God. Anglican Church leaders were touched, and brought the impartation back to Great Britain. From here an American evangelist, Steve Hill, brought the fire to Pensacola, Florida. Brownsville Assembly of God was changed by the glory of God's presence there and thousands have flocked to receive from Him.

In 1975, when God touched me in a powerful way with the baptism in the Holy Spirit, very few shook like me in the presence of the Lord. When I walked into the Toronto church with 5,500 people present, many were shaking with the power of God. The first words I spoke as I entered the place were, "You're back, Lord."

The manifest presence brings a power that can cause a shaking. The word of God says:

When God spoke from Mount Sinai His voice shook the earth, but now He makes another promise: "Once again I will shake not only the earth but the heavens also." This means that the things on earth will be shaken, so that only eternal things will be left. Since we are receiving a Kingdom that cannot be destroyed, let us be thankful and please God by worshipping Him with holy fear and awe, for our God is a consuming fire (Hebrews 12:26-29 NLT).

I see God shaking us now with a new fire of baptism. The manifestation of His presence is leading us to repentance before His holiness and majesty. He is causing the Church to shake off things that need to be shed from the flesh, so that what remains might be pure and holy before the Lord. And what remains will not be shaken when the judgment of the fire comes upon the world.

Sometimes, in the manifested presence of God, a "thickening" of the cloud occurs. This is what is referred to as the glory, or *kabod*. When the glory of God approaches, shoes are taken off, for it is holy ground. God appeared to Moses in the burning bush and told Moses not to come any closer. He then told Moses to take off his sandals, for the place where he was standing was holy ground. God revealed Himself to Moses, and Moses hid his face because he was afraid. This is the feeling that is evoked at the glory of God. This is no time for song, or a spoken word. It is time to bow down and prostrate yourself before him. The very word *kabod* means "weight," so when the glory of God comes, its weight on the flesh becomes so heavy that one cannot stand or even move under the weight of His glory.

The first time I came under the glory of God occurred in Melbourne, Florida in 1995 where the late Christian author Jamie Buckingham had pastored. It is interesting to note that the name of the church was the "Tabernacle." Revival was breaking out in the area. Repentance and unity among clergy brought forth a period of eight months renewal during which thousands of conversions to Christ resulted. During the first week of revival, I found myself face down on the platform of the altar unable to move for well over an hour. I could not move any part of my body, although I was conscious of what was going on around me.

The second time this occurred was in Cleveland, Ohio in 1996, where I was leading a nine month revival meeting five nights a week. As I stood at the pulpit, I literally collapsed on the red brick floor from the sheer weight of the glory. Just before I fell, my words to the people began to slur and came off my tongue slowly and with great effort. Finally, my mouth didn't work anymore. My flesh fell hard to the ground. God shows us He shares the stage with no man. All flesh must bow and die before Him. God is now unmistakably present in His splendor. This experience in Cleveland happened following a deep protracted hunger on the part of hundreds who religiously assembled just to worship Him. The cloud of God's glory followed the praises of His people.

The third time the glory fell on me happened in 1997 while I was ministering in an obscure country church in Indiana. Not many evangelists would go to this church because it was a small congregation. I thought God wanted me to go to them. I obeyed Him. During the service I pointed out a man in the back of the church for a healing. He was crippled with a leg injury. I told him God was more interested in the state of his soul than He was in the state of his leg. I told him that he needed to get his life right with God. So he would know that God meant business with him, I told him God would heal his leg. I prayed for the healing, and the man dropped his crutches and walked by the power of God.

I brought him forward for his salvation. I had the pastor lead the man in prayer for his salvation. As the pastor began the prayer, both men flew backward in opposite directions onto the carpet. The pastor was slain in the Spirit and unconscious for over two hours. During this time the glory of the Lord began to move over the people in the church. Little children, teenagers, mothers, and men wept and repented in the presence of God. God chose this little church of a few hundred to make His habitation.

The church sits off the only major highway from Indianapolis to Cincinnati. God instructed them that He would begin to send people driving along the highway who were in need of help from Him. They were to simply usher those who came into the sanctuary to the habitual presence of the Lord. God would take care of the rest. The morning after the visitation of God people began to drive off the highway to the church. A mother and daughter were the first to come. They were brought into the sanctuary as directed by the Lord. Both felt very uncomfortable in the room, so they tried to leave the church. As they reached for the back door of the church both were slain in the Spirit. The girl was delivered from drugs, and the mother came under the conviction of God.

Inside the Ark of the Covenant

The innermost court of the Tabernacle was called the Holy of Holies or the Most Holy Place. Here is the place where the Ark of the Covenant rested. Inside the Ark were placed three items. These sacred items were the staff of Aaron that budded, the tablets with the Ten Commandments, and the pot of manna from Heaven. Let us take a closer look at these three items.

The history of the budded staff of Aaron is found in Numbers 17. The leaders of Israel gathered in opposition to Moses and Aaron. They were discontented because they found themselves in a desert wilderness. The Lord directed Moses to gather together the 12 staffs of each leader. Their names were written on each staff, and placed in the Tent of Meeting over night. The next day the staff of Aaron had sprouted and budded forth almonds. The staff of Aaron indicated the authority of God. The authority of God led the people of Israel on their way to the Promised Land.

Next, God gave the Ten Commandments to Moses while Moses met with God on Mount Sinai. The first four commandments deal with the nature of God. He is the only God, and His nature is Holy and due reverence and worship by man. The last six commandments deal with human relationship. The laws of these six commandments are given by a loving God to help us in our dealings with one another. These laws set before the people of Israel the standard for truth. A complete listing of the Ten Commandments can be found in Exodus 20:1-17. The Commandments represent the word of God, which is truth.

Thirdly, the pot of manna from Heaven is the manna God supplied to the people each day as they wandered through the desert. This bread from Heaven represents God's provision for the people. God provided fresh manna each day except on the Sabbath day. On the sixth day, they were to gather twice as much, so they might rest on the Sabbath. Exodus 16 records the account of the miracle of the manna. The pot of manna, then, is the bread of life.

I asked the Lord why these items bore so much significance to Him. He said, "They represent My son, Jesus." I asked Him how this was so. He replied, "The three items represent the Way, the Truth, and the Life. The staff of Aaron showed the 'Way' to the children of Israel. The Ten Commandments showed the people the 'Truth.' The bread from Heaven gave the hungry children of Israel 'Life.' God then said to me, "The Ark of the Covenant contained Jesus."

CHAPTER TEN

THE MERCY SEAT (DESTINY REGAINED)

Make an atonement cover of pure gold—two and a half cubits long and a cubit and a half wide. And make two cherubim out of hammered gold at the ends of the cover. Make one cherub on one end and the second cherub on the other; make the cherubim of one piece with the cover, at the two ends. The cherubim are to have their wings spread upward, overshadowing the cover with them. The cherubim are to face each other, looking toward the cover. Place the cover on top of the ark of the Testimony, which I will give you. **There,** *above the cover between the two cherubim that are over the ark of the Testimony,* **I will meet with you** *and give you all My commands for the Israelites (Exodus 25:17-22, emphasis mine).*

We notice there is no wood in its construction because none of it speaks of man, only God. This is the ultimate piece of furniture in the Tabernacle because it represents God's throne of judgment made into a throne of mercy by the shedding of the blood. God accepted the blood of animals under the Old Testament, but under the New Testament the blood of Christ took the place of the blood of animals. The New Testament teaches us:

*For all have sinned and fall short of the glory of God, and are justified freely by His grace through the redemption that came by Christ Jesus. God presented Him as a sacrifice of **atonement** [propitiation or reconciliation] through faith in His blood (Romans 3:23-25a, emphasis mine).*

The Greek word for atonement or propitiation is *hilasterion*, the same word for "Mercy Seat." In other words, Jesus, our atonement, has paid for all our sins in full. Our sin is not simply covered over or pardoned, although this is true. Our sins are remitted; our debt taken away. They no longer exist with God through the blood of Jesus, so they should no longer exist in our minds and hearts. The only memory we should have is the memory of thanksgiving for His great mercy.

The two cherubim are referred to as "cherubim of glory" (see Heb. 9:5). Nowhere are they referred to as angels as other cherubim are identified throughout the word of God. It is likewise significant to identify the structure of the cover as a seat, yet no man ever sits on this throne.

Paul tells us:

Day after day every priest stands and performs his religious duties; again and again he offers the same sacrifices, which can never take away sins. But when this priest had offered for all time one sacrifice for sins, He sat down at the right hand of God (Hebrews 10:11-12).

This signifies the work of Jesus is done, and so He sits on the Mercy Seat for it belongs to Him alone. No more blood was to be sprinkled on this Seat since His blood was sprinkled on it for all time. The Mercy Seat of Jesus is in the middle of the lid. Kevin Conner so beautifully reveals in his book, *The Tabernacle of Moses* (City Bible Publishing, 1976), that the two cherubim of glory represent the Father and the Holy Spirit. The cover of gold with the two cherubim is one solid piece of gold representing the Trinity: One God in three Persons.[xvii]

The Meeting Place

It must be noted that Exodus 25:22 says God would meet them at the Mercy Seat. This is a profound revelation. It is really saying God meets us at the place of mercy. God meets the sinner with a broken and contrite heart.

I would like very much to tell three stories about people in the Bible who illustrate how God meets the sinner with a broken and contrite heart. They further illustrate how the seat of mercy transforms them into passionate lovers of God.

(1) Mary of Bethany:

Now the Passover and the Feast of Unleavened Bread were only two days away, and the chief priests and the teachers of the law were looking for some sly way to arrest Jesus and kill Him. 'But not during the Feast,' they said, 'or the people may riot.' While He was in Bethany, reclining at the table in the home of a man known as Simon the Leper, a woman came with an alabaster jar of very expensive perfume, made of pure nard. She broke the jar and poured the perfume on His head. Some of those present were saying indignantly to one another, "Why this waste of perfume? It could have been sold for more than a year's wages and the money given to the poor." And they rebuked her harshly. "Leave her alone," Jesus said. "Why are you bothering her? She has done a beautiful thing to Me. The poor you will always have with you, and you can help them any time you want. But you will not always have Me. She did what she could. She poured perfume on My body beforehand to prepare for My burial. I tell you the truth, wherever the gospel is preached throughout the world, what she has done will also be told in memory of her" (Mark 14:1-9).

This account of the woman of Bethany is also recorded in Matthew 26:6-13, in Luke 7:36-50, and in John 12:1-8. Bethany was the town of Lazarus, Martha, and Mary who were very close friends to Jesus. Jesus would often go to their home for rest and quiet. The woman in the story of the alabaster jar is possibly Mary of Bethany. The account in Luke says she was a "woman who had lived a sinful life in that town," which means she had been known in the town as an immoral person. She had looked for love in all the wrong places until she met Jesus. She burst into the dining area with her jar of nard, washed His feet with her tears, and dried His feet with her hair. Then she kissed his feet and poured the perfume all over them. Her radical behavior was repulsive, despicable, and obscene to the guests. But to Jesus, it was the most lavish gift of love He had ever received.

When the Pharisee who had invited Him saw this, he said to himself, "If this man were a prophet, he would know who was touching him and what kind of woman she is—that she is a sinner." Jesus answered him, "Simon, I have something to tell you." "Tell Me, teacher," he said. "Two men owed money to a certain moneylender. One owed him five hundred denarii, and the other fifty. Neither of them had the money to pay him back, so he canceled the debts of both. Now which of them will love him more?" Simon replied, "I suppose the one who had the bigger debt canceled." "You have judged correctly," Jesus said. Then He turned toward the woman and said to Simon, "Do you see this woman? I came into your house. You did not give me any water for My feet, but she wet My feet with her tears and wiped them with hair. You did not give Me a kiss, but this woman, from the time I entered, has not stopped kissing My feet. Therefore, I tell you, her sins have been forgiven—for she loved much. But he who has been forgiven little loves little" (Luke 7:39-47).

Whoever is forgiven much by Jesus loves Him much. Whoever is forgiven little by Jesus loves Him little. This is a biblical principle that applied to Mary of Bethany's life. She had to be so aware of her unhappy lifestyle, yet she knew of no way out of it. It had taken her over. Then, in an instant, a different kind of man walked into her life. He looked at her differently from all the others. He peered into her very heart and soul. He saw into her struggle, and called her into a place of health and healing. He respected her as a person and as a woman. He was not interested in using her for His own gain. In a moment He transformed her inestimable measure of lust into passionate, extravagant love.

If one has not known the depth of personal sin, how can one be grateful for forgiveness of it? If people think they are no better or worse than the next, how can they appreciate Jesus' act of forgiveness on the cross? If a person says, "I haven't murdered anyone; I'm not so bad," has this individual reached the point where salvation is even deemed necessary? I am not implying that we need to go out and commit gross sins in order to know God's love.

What I am saying is that we need to recognize our sinful nature without God in order to appreciate His gracious extension of mercy. The word of God says:

> *You have heard that it was said to the people long ago, "Do not murder, and anyone who murders will be subject to judgment." But I tell you that anyone who is angry with his brother will be subject to judgment (Matthew 5:21-22a).*

We must come to the Mercy Seat in need of mercy. We must reach the point where we throw ourselves on the mercy of God. This act of abandonment to Him will lead us to find the Lover of our soul. The consequence of this act of seeking mercy is to find love. *"This is love: not that we loved God, but that He loved us…"* (1 John 4:10). To know, that in spite of what we may have done, we are still loved, is to know love.

It was considered to be an act of defilement in Jewish tradition for a holy man like Jesus to ever be touched by a woman of Mary's reputation. To further complicate matters, Mary's bigger than life behavior with Jesus caused an enormous reaction of personal discomfort and embarrassment from the men present. This would still be a problem for most men today. A public display of affection like Mary showed would be observed as a violation of protocol and even liberal morals. Jesus shows us that the fragrance of Mary's love rose up to Him, as did the fragrance of the sweet smelling perfume. Intimacy can be only had with God by "the breaking open of ourselves" before Him just as the perfume jar was broken open. To withhold our affections, whether in public or in private, is to deny oneself intimacy with the Lover of our soul, and to deny our God the type of love our affections should bring to Him.

(2) Mary Magdalene:

In the Gospel of John, one reads, *"Early on the first day of the week, while it was still dark, Mary of Magdala, went to the tomb and saw that the stone had been removed from the entrance"* (John 20:1). The synoptic gospels identify Mary Magdalene as one *"from whom seven demons had come out"* (Luke 8:2). She had been delivered by Jesus and supported the ministry of Jesus "out of her own means" (see Luke 8:3). She came to the tomb of Jesus early on Sunday morning to anoint the body of Jesus. There wasn't time on Friday to give him a proper burial, since the Jewish Sabbath fast approached at the time Jesus died at three in the afternoon. She came with two other women: Mary, the mother of James the younger, and Salome, the mother of James and John.

Mary saw the large stone rolled back, and her first thought was that the body of Jesus had been taken. She ran to tell the disciples in the upper room, and she returned to the tomb with them crying. After Peter and John left the site for their homes, Mary is still found at the tomb weeping.

As she wept, she bent over to look into the tomb and saw two angels in white, seated where Jesus' body had been, one at the head and the other at the foot. They asked her, "Woman, why are you crying?" "They have taken my Lord away," she said, "and I don't know where they have put Him." At this, she turned around and saw Jesus standing there, but she did not realize that it was Jesus. "Woman," He said, "why are you crying? Who is it you are looking for?" Thinking He was the gardener, she said, "Sir, if you have carried Him away, tell me where you have put Him, and I will get Him." Jesus said to her, "Mary." She turned toward Him and cried out in Aramaic, "Rabboni!" (which means Teacher) (John 20:10-16).

This picture presents an incredible revelation! One would be forced to ask, "Why would Jesus choose to appear first to Mary rather than to Peter or John?" "Why would Jesus appear first to a woman and not a man?" Mary had been "unclean." Seven demons had been cast out of her. Let me try to explain the possible rationale of the Lord.

Recall when Mary peered into the empty burial chamber. The veil of the stone had been rolled away. Inside she saw two angels facing each other, one at either end of the slab of stone on which had laid the Lamb slain for the sin of the world. Jesus had risen from the dead. He had swallowed up sin and death in victory. The empty tomb had become the New Testament Holy of Holies. The two cherubim facing each other upon the blood drenched altar gazed upon the new "Mercy Seat." It is at the Mercy Seat that God says He will meet with us, and it is at the new Mercy Seat that God meets with Mary of Magdalene. The blood of Jesus had been placed on the new Mercy Seat for all humanity for all time. It gives way to the bright promise of immortality. Jesus is risen!

We can join Paul in saying, *"Where, O death, is your victory? Where, O death is your sting? The sting of death is sin, and the power of sin is the law. But thanks be to God! He gives us victory through our Lord Jesus Christ"* (1 Cor. 15:55-57).

This beautiful picture of Christ's love for Mary of Magdalene shows a woman now standing in the place of the Old Testament high priest. He had to be ritually cleansed in order to go into the Most Holy Place. Mary, the "unclean" one, is made holy through Jesus' sacrifice. Mary, the woman, is given preference to men because of her desperate, passionate love for Jesus. She now stands in the bridal chamber of the garden with Jesus her Lover. Pure love has been restored. Jesus makes mention of her name "Mary," and intimacy is regained.

(3) Joseph:

The story of Joseph is a story of a man who kept his heart right before God. In spite of his circumstances he did not harden his heart against his brothers or against the Lord. He kept his eyes upon God's greater sovereignty over his life. He believed God was in control and because Joseph believed his purposes were in God's hand, he was in the right place at the right time.

Sometimes we think we know what is best for us. Sometimes we think we know how things should work out. When they don't go the way expected, we become disturbed and angry. At times we might even get angry with God.

I am not proud of what I did to my relationship with God. He had blessed me in ways unimaginable. We walked in a place of close intimacy and friendship. But following the hurt and pain of persecution and rejection, I walked away from my relationship with Him. Hurt and pain comes to all of us. We all experience emotional pain. I know God made my intellectual and emotional chemistry, and I know a price comes with intensity. I feel very deeply about what I believe. However, it is one thing to feel deeply; it is quite another to blame the very One you thought should protect you from the hurt. Psalm 55:12-14 expresses what it feels like to be hurt by someone close to us:

If an enemy were insulting me, I could endure it; if a foe was raising himself against me, I could hide from him. But it is you, a man like myself, my companion, and my close friend, with whom I once enjoyed sweet fellowship as we walked with the throng at the house of the God.

The pain of betrayal runs deep. When best friends turn their backs on you, and you have no other friend to turn to, it can be devastating enough. But when, with clouded vision, you perceive God betraying you it can seem like an incurable wound. Jeremiah must have felt this way when he said: *"I had been like a gentle lamb led to the slaughter. I did not realize that they had plotted against me. 'Let us destroy the tree and its fruit; let us cut him off from the land of the living, that his name be remembered no more'"* (Jer. 11:19).

I found myself saying with Jeremiah, "O Lord you duped me, and I let myself be duped" (see Jer. 20:7). It is easy to do what I did and turn away from God at times of trial. When people we care about don't react to us the way we had hoped. It is much more difficult to dwell on the promises of God when He says: *"And everyone who has left houses or brothers or sisters or father or mother or children or fields for my sake will receive a hundred times as much and will inherit eternal life"* (Matt. 19:29).

The truth of these words notwithstanding, I left God behind. In the Old Testament, Joseph knew what it was like to be betrayed. He was sold as a slave by the hands of his brothers. He spent ten long years in a cold prison cell. He never gave up on his God, nor did he ever blame his God for his circumstances. Joseph kept close to the Lord through all his pain and trial. He continued to walk with the Lord. We must learn how to keep Jesus on the throne of our hearts. Remember, in the story of Joseph, God gives him two sons. The first is called Manasseh while the second is called Ephraim.

Joseph named his firstborn Manasseh and said, "It is because God has made me forget all my trouble and all my father's household." The second son he named Ephraim and said, "It is because God has made me fruitful in the land of my suffering" (Genesis 41:51-52).

The land of Joseph's suffering was Egypt where Joseph was appointed by Pharaoh to be in charge of the whole land of Egypt. He was in charge of the plentiful granary at a time when famine was widespread in the land. I often wondered why Joseph was rewarded with such a position. I believe it is because Joseph learned the lessons the enemy tries to inflict on good intentioned people. He passed the course with flying colors. Because of his attitude toward his trouble, God rewarded him *"in the land of his suffering."* This amplified Joseph's victory over satan because God blessed him in a land ruled by His enemy.

I was not as wise as Joseph at the time. I remember cursing myself by saying, "I will never allow anyone else to hurt me again." When a person says this, they virtually bind themselves off to the possibility of ever being loved again. There is a magnificent movie called *Shadowlands*, which chronicles the life of C.S. Lewis. Lewis is a well known twentieth century Christian philosopher who explores, among other things, the intense subject of "suffering" in his writings. This passionately, opinionated professor from a world of ideas finds himself embattled with pain when he allows himself to fall in love with a woman who eventually is diagnosed with cancer. This riveting woman, Joy

Gresham, is more than Lewis' match. His once orderly life is turned upside down by the prognosis for his wife. His emotional nerve endings are exposed and raw.

Joy Gresham's death teaches C. S. Lewis love and life. Joy and pain; love and heartache, all come in a package deal. You can't know one without the other. That's the deal!

When we close ourselves off to love, we close ourselves off to life. It was not until we realize it hurts to love, but it hurts much more not to love, that we come to our senses. We need to repent of our sins, renounce the curses we put on ourselves, and return to God.

For me, I found myself getting reacquainted with God again in 1990 with the birth of my son. God showed me His love again, and I felt safe expressing my love to my son. God knew who would be safe for me. I sat there before my little infant boy. In an instant, without ever thinking of it, I transferred all the loving feeling that I had for my son onto a scene in which God took over my place as a Daddy, and I took over my son's place as an infant. Wow! The love was overwhelming, and the tears flooded my soul. Our relationship was restored.

The Prodigal Son

God used the story of the parable of the lost son to touch me. Luke records it in his gospel: Jesus said:

There was a man who had two sons. The younger one said to his father, 'Father, give me my share of the estate.' So he divided his property between them. Not long after that, the younger son got together all he had, set off for a distant country and there squandered his wealth in wild living. After he had spent everything, there was a severe famine in that whole country, and he began to be in need (Luke 15:11-14).

Thank God for a place of need. It is only when we find ourselves at a place of need that we can be saved. Without having a need, we are self-sufficient. Faced with troubles and trials greater than ourselves, we turn to someone else for help. Being brought to a place of need puts us in touch with our own mistakes and sin. This is what happened to the lost son in the parable.

When he came to his senses, he said, "How many of my father's hired men have food to spare, and here I am starving to death! I will set out and go back to my father and say to him: 'Father, I have sinned against heaven and against you. I am no longer worthy to be called your son; make me like one of your hired men.'" So he got up and went to his father (Luke 15:17-20a).

"Coming to his senses" is an expression we use in our language today. All too often we can find ourselves head-strong and wandering into things we shouldn't. We wander "into a distant land" which speaks metaphorically of venturing into sin. Finally, we sometimes realize that where we've gone is wrong and harmful to us. We come to our senses and return home.

"But while he was still a long way off, his father saw him and was filled with compassion for him; he ran to his son, threw his arms around him and kissed him" (Luke 15:20).

The father's reaction is one of love for his son who has returned home. The father doesn't demand an explanation for his son's behavior. The father doesn't say, "I told you so." He simply embraces his son with open arms and welcomes him back home.

The story of the Bible is the perennial story of a loving father pursuing his wayward children. He tries time and time again to woo them back. More than anything else he wants them to know his love for them. It is the ultimate love story of a father who gives it all to this end. The one message he wants to communicate in the pages of the Bible is simply, "I love you."

How utterly ridiculous it is for us to ever think that our faith consists in what we can do for God. Our faith is totally based on what God has done for us. Our faith is not about keeping laws so we can be "nicer than they are" with nicer morals. This would be tantamount to an insult to God and a prostitution of the good news.

The staggering truth of the matter is that God doesn't love us in some vague, philosophical way. He doesn't love us in some esoteric way. Nothing could be further from the truth. God is **Love**! He can do nothing but love by nature. The proof of His love is that He spared not His only begotten Son, Jesus, to suffer and die in our place. Are we worth the death of anyone, least of all God's Son? So every time you scorn yourself or put yourself down, you are saying to God that what He freely died for wasn't worth it. God trusts us enough and believes enough in us to take someone like the hardened, tax collector Levi and transform him into Matthew, the evangelist, or a friendless, wealthy Zacchaeus and transform him into a generous giver.

Like these two men, Jesus saw that I wasn't beyond help. He pursued me like the Hound of Heaven. For 13 years I had walked away from Him. I no longer prayed, rarely went to church, and wasn't even sure that God even existed. I convinced myself God was forever out of my life. But He kept pursuing me. Finally, I gave in to the madness of it all when He said:

"Frank, out of love for you I came to this earth. I allowed Myself to be mocked, scorned, bruised, and beaten. I was nailed to a cross and died. This was all for you, who ran from Me and didn't even want to hear My name ever again. For 13 years I've waited. I've waited for you to call out My name. When I lost you Frank, I lost My best friend."

These words were almost too much for me to take. Who in this world could ever love me like He loves me? Who could ever be as faithful and patient as He has? He reached down to me, unworthy though I am; He reached out to me like no one ever has. At that moment I realized His love is for real and forever. I said to Him, "Lord, never let me leave You again. For my life has no meaning or sense if you are not at its very center."

This is the essence of the good news. Falling in love with One who loves me despite myself. One cannot know the excitement of God until one is penetrated by the forgiving power of Jesus' love that takes us to the forgiving heart of the Father.

This is the core message of evangelical Christianity. It is not about "being good." It is not about trying to please God by repressing our desires to sin in order to be good. The truth is that God comes to unmask every illusion we have created about ourselves. We cannot hide from Him behind fig leaves. God sees right through our awkward attempts at covering ourselves and destroys every icon and false idol that we have ever made. God's love is so great for us that He would never allow false images to keep us apart. He is an unquenchable Lover after our souls.

Some false illusions would have us believe that God torments and teases us. Nothing could be further from the truth. God does not toy with us, or make life more difficult for us. He does not want us to fear Him except with a healthy fear of the Lord that makes us humble servants before the great *I Am*.

Some of us can't handle the gratuitous nature of the Father. Our selfish goals and modus operandi taint us. Think of the parable of the workers in the vineyard. Those workers who went out into the vineyard at the eleventh hour were paid the same wage as those who worked all day long. These then grumbled and complained against the owner because those who worked one hour were paid the same wage as they were paid. The landowner said to the workers who grumbled:

I am not being unfair to you. Didn't you agree to work for a denarius? Take your pay and go. I want to give the man who was hired last the same as I gave you. Don't I have the right to do what I want with my money? Or are you envious because I am generous? (Matthew 20:15)

God is crazy with love. He is insanely generous to those who but look His way. He does not condemn us or judge us. We do that to ourselves. We judge ourselves through our choices for or against Him. God even loves those who hate Him. God even loves those who do evil. The son reigns on the just and on the unjust.

We somehow conspire in our weak unbiblical thinking to make out that God doesn't love us. We come to believe and act that we have to earn His love and earn His approval. I learned God simply takes me as I am. He simply forgives me for my wanderings. That is pure amnesty. God's love is based on nothing that comes from us. If it happened to be based on something that came from us we would certainly find a way of messing it up. All is based on His Son, Jesus. Our responsibility is to say, "thank you."

In 1996, a friend as well as an insightful spiritual writer of the last century died. He had taught at Yale and Harvard universities, but God called him to go to Richmond Hills, Ontario to pastor a small group of mentally and physically challenged individuals. He wondered why God had put this opportunity before him. He said, "But Lord, they haven't read any of my books. What can I teach them?" His name was Henri Nouwen. God replied, "Henri, I'm not sending you there that you might give them anything. I'm sending you there that they might give to you." I had the privilege of getting to know this man just before he died. He learned to have a gentle, humble spirit of love and tender mercy. The mentally challenged people had disarmed him of every defense. He could no longer hide behind academia. His intellect was of little use to the cerebral palsied Adam, his charge. He found himself, in the final analysis, face to face with love.

The old vindictive images of God now give way to an image in keeping with mercy. God cherishes you like no one else, He forgives you in spite of your protestation, and He liberates you from deserved punishment, and calls you to a life with Him in eternity.

The Mercy Seat then is the place where God promises to meet us. We should not fear coming to Him on bended knee. He waits for us every time with open arms to welcome us home. The mercy seat is destiny regained. We are back on track again!

CHAPTER ELEVEN

THE MOST HOLY PLACE (UNION)

Most never seem to step "beyond the veil" into the dimension where Heavenly love is awakened. Not unlike our earthly affections for our earthly bride or groom, going "beyond the veil" stirs us to new heights of love. Here is where a heart is smitten by divine encounter. The lure of God's faint perfume lingers before our heart enough to cause us to run after Him for another day. Its memory, however, though it fades, never ceases to be a memory of love's greatest moment in time. This memory intact is enough to engage our desires for just another wisp of His fragrant presence.

To move beyond the veil is to enter into the dimension of sacrament. Here we experience the union of the human with the divine. It is a place of sacred encounter.

Marriage

Marriage has been called a sacrament. A sacrament is an outward sign of an inner reality. As husband and wife are joined together in marriage their relationship declares to all that they are outwardly joined together by an inner vow of love. This inner vow speaks to the reality that the two take each other in a definable and mutual commitment for better or for worse until death due them part. They become a living testimony to their love relationship, announcing that whatever might come their way, they will mingle their lives as one. They announce to the world that whoever they are, whatever they can become, they will discover themselves within this unique bond of love. The promise is made to be a helpmate who willingly is committed to accept, respect, nurture, correct in love, forgive, and delight in the other. Such promise demands grace in order to enter into the mutual progress of each spouse's development.

Marriage is both practical and spiritual at the same time. Likewise, true love is both practical and spiritual at the same time. Love seeks to give by nature and by essence. Its sole desire is to see another receive enjoyment, satisfaction, and pleasure. Love gives, and its reward comes in the form of seeing its object fulfilled. In marriage, a husband and wife experience this level of love by bringing feelings of delight and pleasure. These feelings evoke a deeper desire to be in union with each other.

The Song of Songs in the Bible unfolds a dramatic sensual account of two lovers caught up in sacramental love for each other. The story describes in intimate detail the longings of the couple to be together. Separation makes them heartsick; union makes them lovesick. Here one contemplates a wistful relationship of a husband and wife. Its allegory is spiritually pure and wholesome; its history is practical and predictable at the same time. It is a story as old as love itself but spoken from the mind of unparalleled love.

In Song of Songs, one finds the Shulammite woman longing for her lover as she describes him to the women:

My lover is radiant and ruddy, outstanding among ten thousand. His head is purest gold; his hair is wavy and black as a raven. His eyes are like doves by the water streams, washed in milk, mounted like jewels. His cheeks are like beds of spice yielding perfume. His lips are like lilies dripping with myrrh. His arms are rods of gold set with chrysolite. His body is like polished ivory decorated with sapphires. His legs are pillars of marble set on bases of pure gold. His appearance is like Lebanon, choice as its cedars. His mouth is sweetness itself; he is altogether lovely. This is my lover, this is my friend, O daughters of Jerusalem (Song of Songs 5:10-16).

The Shulammite opens our eyes to the passion she has for her beloved, the Bridegroom. Entering into the Holy of Holies erases any other desire in the world, and it causes one to focus solely on the pursuit of Jesus. With the veil folded back, one now beholds Him as He is. With fervency awakened, one sets out in a direction, which will hopefully lead to future encounters with His beauty. Now the realization clearly defines that all else is vain pursuit. Once He has captured the heart, there is no turning back for vain pursuits. The only true passion is for Him. When He withdraws His presence, it is to further our pursuit. Like the game, hide and seek, He tests our affections toward Him. Even in the midst of the trials of life, the Shulammite woman in love is self-possessed. She is able to step back out of her immediate crisis and recognize His love for her overarches her problems. His love for her is constant and enduring.

The chase after God cannot be set in motion by any other way than by the touch of Jesus. The incarnate reality of His presence meets us face to face in life's troubles and sin. God and man at table are sat down. Boundless, endless Love comes crashing in, to lift us in our true weakness. Jesus, and only Jesus, turns our affections toward God. The young woman in love again says:

Let him kiss me with the kisses of his mouth, for your love is more delightful than wine. Pleasing is the fragrance of your perfumes; your name is like perfume poured out. No wonder the maidens love you! Take me away with you. Let us hurry! The king has brought me into his chambers (Song of Songs 1:2-4).

Jesus, the Lover of her soul, has captured her heart. He takes her into the chambers of God. Yes, it is true the Most Holy Place is a place of awe, fear and trembling. But it is likewise the place of the marriage chamber.

Some believers and churches emphasize the transcendence of God in His awesome power and glory. Other believers and churches center their understanding of God on a spirit of familiarity and blessing. Neither is totally correct, nor are they totally wrong. Here, the Spirit of God reveals an intimate dimension of passionate love as seen on the marriage bed of two newlywed lovers.

Passion

Mike Bickle, in his book *Passion for Jesus*, declares that the word of God is about God's plans for humankind, but also about God's plans for His Son.[xviii] God says:

> *I will proclaim the decree of the Lord: He said to me, "You are my Son; today I have become your Father. Ask of me, and I will make the nations your inheritance, the ends of the earth your possession. You will rule them with an iron scepter; You will dash them to pieces like pottery" (Psalm 2:7-9).*

Bickle writes about a twofold inheritance both for man and for Jesus. Our inheritance is to experience love from a passionate God. Jesus is to experience His inheritance as our passionate love for Him. This will be realized only as we become radically committed to Him. Psalm 2:10-12 commands us to be wise and, *"Kiss the Son, lest He be angry..."* Passionate affections are then necessary to enter into God's inheritance for us and for His Son. Some think the text is referring to courtly protocol. I think rather the Holy Spirit is referring to passion. The symbolic language used here should be a catalyst to rouse our souls toward God. One way or another, our passions, our allegiance, our loyalties are roused for someone or something in this world. Someone or something wins our pleasures in life. Let them be toward God!

Pursuit of all other passions still leads to an inner emptiness. Nothing in this world can fill the void and longing of our soul. God made us to be complete only in Him. He wants us to be filled up with Him. Saint Augustine

(354-430) understood this truth many years ago. He wrote against the skeptics who believed that truth was elusive and unattainable. Augustine believed it was man's nature to seek after truth, and that one does not rest until he rests in the truth of finding God. The object of desire is the God revealed to us in the Bible.

Saint Augustine was led to this conclusion by personal experience after pursuing a life of self-indulgence. The lusting desires of his flesh left him empty and dissatisfied. It wasn't until his conversion and newfound faith that he was able to receive peace into his restless soul. This transformation of his soul left Augustine illuminated, as if his soul were brightened with a divine light to see what was absolutely good and true.

Augustine discovered his identity was in God. He was made for the pleasures of God. His heart could finally rest because it rested in Him. In Song of Songs 7:10 we read, *"I belong to my lover, and His desire is for me."* Augustine, like countless others, found this statement to be true. Our identity and self-acceptance are found in Him. Failure to negotiate this passage in life leaves one a prisoner of the continual search for one's identity and self-acceptance.

Entering into the person and personality of Jesus by opening up our affections for Him leaves us with little more meaningful to do than desire to possess more of Him. This call goes out in particular for all that walk about in the Holy Place. One will soon find out that pursuing the gifts pale to pursuing the giver. There is an open call to those that know their sins are pardoned in the Outer Court but hardly realize there is so much more awaiting them. To enter into the Holiest of sanctuaries is to live in a conjugal union with Him.

Sometimes, this subject matter seems to shock some individuals. But God is very clear about His thoughts and feelings regarding conjugal love. Sex in the context of marriage is good. God created sex in marriage. The marriage bed is a holy place in the sight of God. Hebrews 13:4 says, *"Marriage is honorable in all, and the bed undefiled"* (NKJV). Sexual intimacy with one's spouse is a time of unfolding revelation into the personality of our spouse. At times it even has the effect of stepping into the personality of our spouse. Proverbs 5:18,19 says, *"Let your fountain be blessed, and rejoice with the wife of your youth...Let her breasts satisfy you at all times, and always be enraptured with her love"* (NKJV). Some may be surprised by God's openness toward sex.

But the truth of the matter is that it would be difficult to understand God on the topic of union without reference to marital union. From the beginning God made man and woman naked before Him and each other. He saw that what He created in "man and woman" was not simply "good" like the rest of creation, but "very good" (Gen. 1:31). The relationship of sex that God designed is without shame for we are *"fearfully and wonderfully made"* (Ps. 139:14).

What keeps the marital relationship alive and well is the fact that the two lives within marriage should not remain static and unchanged. Sexual relations need to be creative and changing in meaning and in practice. When routine sets in, chances are the couple has lost sight of the wonder in each other's gaze. Revival of affections is in order in such an instance. When practice reverts to mechanical routine, affectations need to be awakened. A fresh vitality needs to be discovered in each other. Relationship is constantly changing, so are the needs of the lovers. This means that being attentive to the individual needs of our lover will uncover fresh vitality and life for the marriage.

It would be unrealistic to think that the marital relationship consists in one long love infatuation. No. Every relationship has its ebbs and flows, its disappointments and strains. It is simply the reassuring commitment and covenant that at times manages to pull us through. When love wanes, the decision to love carries us forward. At these times we are sustained in the knowledge that love binds us together despite the lack of reassuring signs.

Bride and Bridegroom

Marital relationship and conjugal love are a beautiful depiction of His affections toward us. We find ourselves as believers in wedded relationship with Christ our Bridegroom. In order to understand this analogy of Bride and Bridegroom it may be important for men to see beyond the connotation of gender. The apostle John understood this connotation to mean a place of "privileged position." It did not connote gender as in masculine or feminine. For a man to be called part of the Bride of Christ simply means that he is in a privileged position with Jesus. John the apostle whom Jesus loved rested his head upon the bosom of Jesus. As they reclined at table celebrating the Passover Feast, Jesus reveals to John that one of the disciples is about to betray Him.

Leaning back against Jesus, [John] asked Him, "Lord, who is it?" Jesus answered, "It is the one to whom I will give this piece of bread when I have dipped it in the dish." Then, dipping the piece of bread, He gave it to Judas Iscariot, son of Simon. As soon as Judas took the bread, Satan entered into him (John 13:25-27).

The ritual dipping that Jesus refers to is the *maror*, or horseradish, and the *kharoset*, or brown apple mixture. At Passover each takes a piece of the unleavened bread and dips it first into the bitter herbs then into the sweet chopped apples with honey signifying that even our most bitter circumstances can be sweetened by the hope we have in God. Jesus willingly allowed two events to take place here. He allowed John to touch His very heartbeat in intimacy while at the same time He allowed Judas to distance his heart by turning it over to satan. In giving the matzah to Judas, His betrayer, He held on to the hope in God.

For the Church to be the Bride of Christ, our hearts must rest on the very heart of Jesus. To know the rhythm and movement of God is key to following His beckoning call. He woos us emotionally and wins us over in complete undivided loyalty. Just as the groom woos and wins over his bride, so too does Jesus woo His Church. I am certain John never wanted to forget that moment of privileged position. His own heart must have felt the warming touch of the Divine setting him ablaze with passionate fire. It was that warmth and fire, which branded John into the service of His Lord, fulfilling the powerful longings pronounced by the Shulammite: *"Set me as a seal upon Your heart, like a seal on Your arm; for love is as strong as death, its jealousy unyielding as the grave. It burns like blazing flame, like a mighty flame"* (Song of Sol. 8:6).

Like John, our ravished, bridal hearts are sealed only for Him. No other one can steal our love away. We become signed and sealed for our eternal destiny and purpose. As we linger in the chambers of our beloved the holiness of God permeates our beings. The process of marinating causes us to carry the scent and fragrance of the one we love. Ravished by His heart, our obsession craves more and more of Love Divine.

There are moments like these when His heart and our heart beat in synchronistic tones of melody. Though they may be rare, they are cherished and indelibly engraved upon our soul. Here, time departs. Here, words are suspended. Here, love yields to a blanket of contentment. Gazing into His radiant eyes is all that exists. Hanging somewhere between Heaven and earth, our weakening flesh pulls us back from orbit. But our consciousness covets the only real moment of truth there is, till His return once more.

The Bride of Christ is in preparation. She is being revived and is beginning to take on her own proper glow.

One reason He has tapped me out to rejoin the ranks of ministry after a 20 year hiatus is because Jesus clearly told me to "dress and adorn His Bride." Healing and miracles will awaken the Bride to her true glory. Healing and miracles will mend the broken heart; proclaim liberty to captives, recovery of sight to the blind, release to those in bondage, and a year of favor from our God.

Recently, my beautiful wife, Eileen, presented me with a music tape from "Friends of the Bridegroom." On this anointed production is poetry by Gary Wiens. I choose to include his thoughts in my book because he captures what I feel when caught up with the Groom. Rarely, has anyone spoken the words of soul like he has.

A wispy fleeting phantom longing, grazes the edges of my soul just out of sight. A faint perfume, it hangs mid-air.

A memory not quite complete touching feelings, stirring something not quite there yet real, O so real.

O sweet Jesus, how long until once more Your gaze arrests my heart.

You come and go, now touching, now keeping distance, unpredictable Like breathe of wind, where can I find You?

Will You be captured as You have captured me?

You've ruined me, You know, for anything else Longing for one vocation fills my soul, to consider You, to feel You, to worship You, to find words, O vain and futile task, that capture what is burning in my heart.

Your gaze presses in upon me, warm yet weighty, on the edge between tender and terrible.

And the oldest truth I know comes back again in plain yet haunting tones, "You love me...I matter to You... and You are never not there."[xix]

Renaissance of the Soul

The world about us is in grave need for a renaissance of the soul, a rebirth in the fires of the Ancient of Days. Contemporary therapists like me hear, at regular, interval stories beleaguered by emptiness, meaninglessness, and disillusionment. People by the scores strive with excessive measure for soulish food of false report. The true bread of life is found in no other but in Him. True soul is revived in love, attachment, and community. One touch from Him, one moment in His presence, one whisper from His voice can transform any longing heart. It is my prayer that the seekers of this world would be open to hear from the Lover of their soul.

The gospel of Matthew records Jesus taking Peter, James, and John up a high mountain:

There He was transfigured before them. His face shone like the sun, and His clothes became as white as the light. Just then there appeared before them Moses and Elijah, taking with Jesus. Peter said to Jesus, "Lord, it is good for us to be here. If You wish, I will put up three shelters—one for You, one for Moses, and one for Elijah." While he was still speaking, a bright cloud enveloped them, and a voice from the cloud said, "This is My Son, whom I love; with Him I am well pleased. Listen to Him!" When the disciples heard this, they fell facedown to the ground, terrified. But Jesus came and touched them. "Get up," He said. "Don't be afraid." When they looked up, they saw no one except Jesus (Matthew 17:2-8).

To enter into the Most Holy Place is to go up a high mountain to be with the Lord. There, forsaking all else, one witnesses a transfiguration. The Jesus we are familiar with in the gospel pages, the Jesus with the same humanity as a brother, now transforms into His Heavenly glory. In the depth of prayer, in the secret place, a mountaintop experience can occur. The brightness of His radiance, the majesty of His power causes even Moses and Elijah to bow down and kiss the Son. Those whose appetites are wetted for His transfiguration can anticipate the day of the New Jerusalem as seen by John the revelator:

Then I saw a new heaven and a new earth, for the first heaven and the first earth had passed away, and there was no longer any sea. I saw the Holy City, the New Jerusalem, coming down out of heaven from God, prepared as a Bride beautifully dressed for her husband. And I heard a loud voice from the throne saying, "Now the dwelling of God is with men, and He will live with them" (Revelation 21:1-3).

Part Four
Stepping Out With God

CHAPTER TWELVE

THE TABERNACLE (TABERNACLES AMONG THEM)

Toward the beginning of John's gospel we read: *"The Word became flesh, and made His dwelling among us. We have seen His glory, the glory of the One and Only, who came from the Father, full of grace and truth"* (John 1:14).

God's presence became a human being in the person of Jesus Christ. Jesus is the visible revelation of the invisible God. God becomes man. Divinity is incarnate in flesh. In the Old Testament God's presence was found in the Tabernacle. Now God's presence is found in the humanity of Jesus. God takes up His dwelling place in Jesus our Savior. The imagery of the Tabernacle continues into the New Testament as the glory of God "pitches His tent" among us. Jesus is the embodiment of God's presence in humanity. When we see Jesus, we see God. Everything of God is reflected in the Lord Jesus Christ. Jesus is God's Tabernacle in the earth.

Some in the Church today are aware that God is doing something new. He seeks to raise up a new order of things. This new order includes a new understanding of the

Tabernacle in us to hold the glory of God. As the Tabernacle of His presence is being fashioned, the old infrastructures in the Church may have difficulty knowing what to do. This presents a problem and a challenge to the Church to be flexible and adaptive. What God is creating in us today may not have been seen in the past on the scale that it will come forth.

To accomplish this sovereign work, one thing God is doing in the Church today is killing religion. He hates religion for religion's sake. He hates empty incantation. He hates a proud spirit that the self-righteous carry. This mentality leaves one with the feeling that one is doing something for God. Its' reductionism leads to a belief that keeping to law, rule, tradition, and the time honored status quo makes one "better than" the other in the sight of God. It has a tendency to look down upon anyone else in a condescending manner. Religion in this sense kills the Spirit because it tries to control the Spirit.

The Spirit of God will not be controlled. He blows when and where He wills. One moment He is here, but as soon as one tries to capture Him, He is gone. By nature He is free. He can be invited and wooed through our attempts to praise Him, but ultimately it is His choice to come into our midst. Nicodemus, a Pharisee and learned man in religion, struggled with understanding the nature of the Spirit of God. Jesus instructed him that he must be born again to enter into the kingdom of God. Nicodemus tried to understand, but his learning got in the way of his ability to perceive. He replied to Jesus:

"How can a man be born when he is old?" Nicodemus asked. "Surely he cannot enter a second time into his mother's womb to be born!" Jesus answered, "I tell you the truth, unless a man is born of water and the Spirit, he cannot enter the kingdom of God. Flesh gives birth to flesh, but the Spirit gives birth to Spirit. You should not be surprised at My saying, 'You must be born again.' The wind blows wherever it pleases. You hear its sound, but you cannot tell where it comes from or where it is going. So it is with everyone born of the Spirit"
(John 3:3-8).

A religion of works can never make one "born-again" of the Spirit. It can only produce more flesh. The Spirit drives those who hear the sound of the Spirit. Structure may not be clear and evident, but His direction is sure. Many have a need to follow concrete structure and clear rules. To walk by the Spirit of God means to be guided by the Spirit of God. God promised not to leave His people orphaned. He provides the Counselor or Advocate of the Holy Spirit to guide us into the way of truth, and to discern for us the ways of evil.

Forerunners

I believe the new order of believer the Lord is calling forth is according to the pattern of John the Baptist. Isaiah prophesied about his coming when he said:

I will send my messenger ahead of you, who will prepare your way. A voice of one calling in the desert, 'Prepare the way for the Lord, make straight paths for Him.' And so John came, baptizing in the desert region and preaching a baptism of repentance for the forgiveness of sins. The whole Judean countryside and all the people of Jerusalem went out to him. Confessing their sins, they were baptized by him in the Jordan River. John wore clothing made of camel's hair, with a leather belt around his waist, and he ate locusts and wild honey. And this was his message: "After me will come one more powerful than I, the straps of whose sandals I am not worthy to stoop down and untie. I baptize you with water, but He will baptize you with the Holy Spirit (Mark 1:2-8).

Jesus called John *"the greatest man born of woman"* (see Matt. 11:11). He was the greatest of prophetic voices in history. Jesus said John the Baptist was a forceful man who took the Kingdom of God by storm (see Matt. 11:12). He called him *"Elijah who was to come"* (see Matt. 11:14). Zechariah, the priest according to the line of Aaron, was John's father. Elizabeth, a descendent of Aaron the high priest, was John's mother. Zechariah was chosen by lot to perform the duty of a priest to burn incense in the Temple of the Lord. Worshipers were assembled in prayer as Zechariah performed his sacerdotal privilege.

The word of God says Zechariah had a supernatural encounter:

An angel of the Lord appeared to him, standing at the right side of the Altar of Incense. When Zechariah saw him, he was startled and was gripped with fear. But the angel said to him: 'Do not be afraid, Zechariah; your prayer has been heard. Your wife Elizabeth will bear you a son, and you are to give him the name John. He will be a joy and a delight to you, and many will rejoice because of his birth, for he will be great in *the sight of the Lord. He is never to take wine or other fermented drink, and he will be filled with the Holy Spirit even from birth. Many of the people of Israel will he bring back to the Lord their God. And he will go on before the Lord, in the spirit and power of Elijah, to turn the hearts of the fathers to their children and the disobedient to the wisdom of the righteous—**to make ready a people prepared for the Lord***" (Luke 1:11-17, emphasis mine).

As Zechariah filled the golden censer with sweet smelling incense, he received a prophetic word from the Lord that his barren wife Elizabeth would bear a son. John would be the first prophet in over four hundred years. His only purpose and goal was to trumpet his voice as the forerunner of the Lord Jesus Christ. Even well before John was born in the sixth month of Elizabeth's pregnancy, he leaped in the womb of his mother at the visitation of Mary, Elizabeth's cousin, who was carrying Jesus as her own child. John's whole spirit and purpose resounded with joy at the coming of the Lord while even in the womb.

When John advanced into full time ministry, he pointed out, *"the Lamb of God who takes away the sins of the world"* (John 1:29). This is significant because John had the legal and spiritual heritage as high priest of his day. Both his mother and father were in the lineage of Aaron the high priest as a direct descendent. Caiaphas, the High Priest of the day, was appointed by the government and had no bloodline with which to claim authority as high priest. He had the title, but lacked the privilege. John lacked the title, but had the privilege. Be wary of those with title, which lack the privilege. What is seen and evident is not always what is spiritual authority. It was the function of the high priest to choose the lamb for sacrifice on the day of Passover. John, the Godly appointed priest, pointed to the Lamb of sacrifice for the sins of the whole world.

John prepared for the first coming of the Lord, and we of this present generation are given the same mandate to prepare for the second coming of the Lord. God is preparing a people for His return. This preparation occurs, as each one of us is willing to step through the pattern of the Tabernacle given by God.

He must change us to be a priest in the order of Melchizedek. The Genesis account states that Melchizedek was a king of righteousness who ruled over Salem (Jerusalem) and blessed Abraham about 2085 BC (see Gen. 14:18-20). The significance here is that the Aaronic priesthood is destined to be set aside, while Melchizedek's priesthood had a "timeless" element to it like that of Jesus' priesthood (*Revell's Bible Dictionary* 1990). xx

I believe we are the generation that will witness the return of the Lord Jesus. The Bible clearly teaches:

Learn a lesson from the fig tree. When its buds become tender and its leaves begin to sprout, you know without being told that summer is near. Just so, when you see the events I've described beginning to happen, you can know His return is near, right at the door. I assure you, this generation will not pass from the scene before all these things take place (Matthew 24:32-34 NLT).

The fig tree is a reference to the people of Israel (see Hos. 9:10). In 1948, the fig tree began to bud as Israel became a nation. This represents the first time the people of Israel have been a nation since their dispersion almost 2000 years ago. The birth of the Jewish people as a nation has monumental implications and significance in prophecy.

I will bring back my exiled people Israel; they will rebuild the ruined cities and live in them. They will plant vineyards and drink their wine; they will make gardens and eat their fruit. I will plant Israel in their own land, never again to be uprooted from the land I have given them," says the Lord your God (Amos 9:14-15).

These are days the Lord refers to as days in which the plowman and the planter will overtake the reaper by the one treading grapes. What He means is that in the end days, as these things begin to take place, the time it will take for things to be accomplished by God will be quickened and speed ahead as if fast-forwarded.

As we look to the daily news, we see the overt assault against this tiny nation in the Middle Eastern world. This attempt to annihilate the nation of Israel runs deeper than the surface players involved. It is an assault engineered by demonic forces because their knowledge tells them Jesus is coming soon. This indicates their time is nearly over.

Therefore prophesy concerning the land of Israel and say to the mountains and hills, to the ravines and valleys: "This is what the Sovereign Lord says: 'I speak in My jealous wrath because

*you have suffered the scorn of the nations.' Therefore this is
what the Sovereign Lord says: 'I swear with uplifted hand
that the nations around you will also suffer scorn. But you, O
mountains of Israel, will produce branches and fruit for My
people Israel, for they will soon come home. I am concerned for
you and will look on you with favor; you will be plowed and
sown, and I will multiply the number of people upon you, even
the whole house of Israel'"* (Ezekiel 36:6-10).

We don't have to go back in memory too far to recall
the Nazi attempt at genocide of the Jewish people.
Although over 6 million Jews were exterminated in the
name of purifying the earth, God's sovereign hand moved
after World War II to establish Israel as a state nation. In
recent years, about 800,000 Jewish people from the former
communist state of the Soviet Union in the north migrate
to their homeland around Jerusalem. A current movement
awaiting the coming of Messiah is drawing the people back
to their land. The day is close before us when the spiritual
eyes of the Jewish people will be unveiled to see Yeshua as
Messiah. *"...And they will look on Him whom they have
pierced; and mourn for Him as one mourns for an only son..."*
(Zech. 12:10 NASB).

I believe we are the "forerunner generation," like John
the Baptist, who will point to the Lord Jesus. Most baby
boomers were born since the time of Israel's birth as a
nation. We are to be God's forerunners born out of the
spirit of John and Elijah to usher in the coming of God.
God is calling for us to be ready for His return.

In Matthew 25, one finds the parable of the ten wise
virgins. The parable demonstrates the need for advanced

preparation and foresight for the return of the Bridegroom. Those wedded to the Groom must have their lamps burning with oil and their wicks trimmed. This represents a sobering picture of a spiritual reality. One may be a virgin (without sin), one may have a lamp (gifted in the Spirit), but if it isn't burning brightly with plenty of oil, one may not be aware of the return of the Bridegroom. This simply means we need to be awake for His return. We need to be aware of the signs of the times.

The parable encourages that we become extravagant lovers of God, a people who look and feel like a Bride in waiting. Until this time, the Church has not looked like a suitable partner for His Son. In Genesis 2:18, the Father told Jesus He would prepare a suitable partner for Him. Saint Paul recognized this revelation, and cried out ecstatically, *"This is a profound mystery—but I am talking about Christ and the church"* (Eph. 5:32).

It is not my intention to advocate some kind of elitist church group. I am not implying that a group should splinter off and run for the mountains for His return. God works through His Church as human and fallible as it is; therefore, we are to work within the Church. We need to come along side our pastors and church leadership. We need to encourage others wherever we can that God can and desires to transform us by His holiness. Likewise, I am not an alarmist crying out "The sky is falling." But to be blind to the possibility that Jesus could be returning soon is to allow worldly matters to anesthetize, causing us to fall asleep. This is precisely what Jesus warns us about.

I came across the true story of a Methodist leader of one of the early American revivals by the name of John Fletcher in *The Life of Smith Wigglesworth* (Ann Arbor:Vine Publications, 1988). Fletcher said:

Lord, I stand in need of oil. My lamp burns dimly. It burns more like smoking flax than a burning and shining light. O quench it not; raise it to a new flame. I want a power from on High. I want to be clothed with a power from on High. I want a penetrating lasting unction of the Holy Spirit. I want my vessel full of oil. I want a lamp of heavenly illumination, a fire of divine love burning day and night in my heart. I want a full application flowing over my body. Baptize me, O God, with a fresh anointing of fire and oil, send the fire, Lord.[xxi]

Ezekiel captures in a lucid description the type of sons and daughters God is raising up for this hour and generation.

The appearance of the living creatures was like burning coals of fire or like torches. Fire moved back and forth among the creatures; it was bright, and lightening flashed out of it. The creatures sped back and forth like flashes of lightening (Ezekiel 1:13-14).

This is a vision of Heavenly things, however; it can be seen as a vision of earthly vessels anointed with the word of God, flashing about with lightening going forth from the mouth of the saints.

Some strain to see with dim eyes what lies ahead for the Church. Some see the future muddled in dark mystery.

Some await a time of tribulation or the moment of the rapture. I believe God has no intention for our future to be gripped in darkness and fear. God gives us no instruction to wait for rapture or tribulation. He clearly reveals His plans and purposes for our future:

And He made known to us the mystery of His will according to His good pleasure, which He purposed in Christ, to be put into effect when the times will have reached their fulfillment—to bring all things in heaven and on earth together under one head, even Christ (Ephesians 1:9-10).

God's purposes and plans are to reveal the glory of the sons of God. We are moving into the time of the unfolding of the sons of God. Those in the Old Testament saw the glory of God at a distance. Those in the New Testament see the glory of God up close as a fire within us. Second Thessalonians 1:10 says, "...*He comes to be glorified in His holy people and to be marveled among all those who have believed.*" The glory of God will dwell in some of us. His radiance and splendor will shine out. God's glory will be beheld again. His divine integrity requires this to be done. The unsaved world will look at last on Him, and reject the horrors of hell. Those living for Him at the end of the age will see His manifested glory revealed in them!

God's Recycle Bin

Let me share a word of encouragement to seasoned warriors of another day and time. There are multitudes of men and women who, like myself, once ministered mightily in the Lord. Circumstances may have led them to be placed on the sidelines or even out of commission for a number of years. Disenchantment, disillusionment, hurt, and rejection all contributed to steering you in another direction.

The God of mercy is looking for prodigals to come home to His call. Beaten down, and burnt out warriors are to be given a second call. Those once on fire, which left ministry for a safer, more respectable career, will be prompted to return. Those who once served on the front lines are summoned to re-enlist. The Lord says to you, "Come back to Me with your whole heart." Jesus wants you to know He misses you. He desires to have you back with Him. He will stir up the embers that have all but died out. He will stir up your passion and your gifts.

Moses questioned God when God called him back into service. Moses felt useless to God because of his sin. Moses questions God, *"Who am I that I should go to Pharaoh and bring the Israelites out of Egypt?"* (Exod. 3:11). Moses saw himself as a "has been," but God saw something else. God dug into His recycle bin and pulled out a mature and ready Moses. Moses, who once had privilege and position in the house of Pharaoh, now had lost himself in order to find himself. The external trappings of persona gave way to the internal realities of God's grace. Moses was now ready for recycling. Let me say something to you. The word of God teaches us, *"Unless a kernel of wheat falls to the ground and dies, it remains only a single seed. But if it dies, it produces many seeds"* (John 12:24).

You, like Moses, are seasoned for what is about to happen all over the world. God is calling you back as a prodigal to be His sickle to reap an end-time harvest for Him. The power of God is made perfect in human weakness. Nobody knows human weakness like you. You who once ministered in power and fell from grace through sin know the fragile nature you step in. You don't need to be reminded that it is God's power at work in you, and not your power at work. You know all too well humility because you once were so familiar with your pride. In your second chance from God, you go after Him rather than the gifts, which you went after the first time around. This time with Saint Paul you will be able to say, *"I consider them all rubbish, that I may gain Christ and be found in Him…"* (Phil. 3:8b-9a).

When God called me back into ministry after nearly 15 long years of virtual absence, I began to leave behind a business and career I had created and built. God made it clear that in order to follow Him "the nets must be dropped" before following Him. In Exodus 34:10, God calls Moses into covenant as He calls us into covenant. He promises:

I am making a covenant with you. Before all your people I will do wonders never before done in any nation in all the world. The people you live among will see how awesome is the work that I, the Lord, will do for you (Exodus 34:10).

If we obey Him, His provision, power, and blessing will follow. He promises that His miraculous work will go before us. Our commitment must be to Him completely because He is a jealous God (see Exod. 34:14). He indicates our heart must be undivided. Our service and devotion must be unswerving. When you drop your nets to follow Him, a new paradigm of life begins to take over. It is like the tectonic plates of an earthquake shifting underneath one's feet. New interests, new priorities, and new vision are cast. He truly becomes the pearl of great price. Passion regained, our motivation is driven toward a noble end: "Your all for Jesus."

Rapture, Tribulation or Something More

This is not a time to be waiting to be rescued from judgment. It is not a time to be raptured away from the work of the harvest that is before us. Rapture will come but not before the sons and daughters of God are revealed. Jesus will return but not before the Bride appears in all of her splendor. Most importantly, God's final plans for the world will be accomplished through his end-time warriors. A harvest will be won for Jesus Christ that is worthy of His dying on the cross! We haven't even begun to see such harvest pouring in for Him.

When the recent outpouring to the Holy Spirit began again on a widespread scale in 1994 in Toronto, Canada, songwriter and worshipper David Ruis wrote a song called "Let Your Glory Fall." It is a clarion call for all touched by the Spirit of God to carry His banner out to the nations. Twenty-five years ago God's Spirit breathed upon me to "carry His banner out to the nations." It is the same yearning that He stirs in thousands of others. The words of the song say:

Father of creation, unfold Your sovereign plan
raise up a chosen generation
that will march through the land.
All creation is longing for the unveiling of power
Would You release Your anointing
O God let this be the hour.
Ruler of the nations, the world has yet to see,
The full release of Your promise,
The church in victory.

Last year, while I was quietly worshiping at a meeting before the Lord, a deeply prophetic woman was dancing beautifully before her King with a scarf that was gold in color with numerous stars embossed all over it. She put the scarf over me at one point. She then spoke the words, "The nations," over and over again. She said, "As Abraham was the father of many nations, so shall your offspring be as numerous as the stars in the heavens." I know God's call and appointments are irrevocable. This word of truth applies to all of you who once had a call to the nations. Perhaps there are those reading along who are to join in the call to return.

Qualities of the Forerunner

Those who dare to press on into the Most Holy Place will take on the mold of the forerunner. They die to self-interest and find that in Him they live and move and have their being. Jesus living within them is their only real issue.

Their bodies are truly temples or containers of His Presence. Forerunners are the new Arks bearing the holiness of God.

There are committed people in every generation that bear the marks of the forerunner. These people are to be multiplied by the thousands and tens of thousands in this hour. People like John the Baptist, Peter and Paul the apostles will light up the face of the earth for Christ Jesus their Lord. They are committed to pressing in to the Most Holy Place to receive all that can be received. One such forerunner of the past century was John G. Lake. He lived by "pressing into" God. He stepped through the Tabernacle into the Holy of Holies because he wouldn't be satisfied with less. This pastor and evangelist wanted more of what God could give him. Lake was a man of extraordinary faith and boldness. People who knew him recount in books his many encounters with the supernatural.

Lake had returned to Spokane, Washington, where he lived, and received news that his secretary, Mrs. Graham, had taken seriously ill. He went to her home and was met at the door by a minister who told Lake that she had already died. Did that stop John G. Lake? No. He continued into the house, climbed the stairs and was met by a woman who told Lake she died almost a half hour ago. Did that stop John G. Lake? No. He went in the bedroom to see the body of Mrs. Graham lying there. He thought about how the Lord loved this woman; how the Lord took her three years before, following a complete hysterectomy in surgery, and gave her back her womb and her ovaries.

He then realized that she had gone on to marry and conceive a child in full health.

Something began to stir in the man of God. His heart was fanned into flame; he picked the body off the bed and called upon God Almighty for the lightening of Heaven to blast the power of death and hell out of her. He commanded her to come back into her body and stay. She returned from the dead and lived! God is looking for a forerunner who will not be moved by circumstances, but recognize the authority God Almighty places within.

Until now we have only experienced brief flashes of God's brilliant power in the earth. We labor as it were to give birth to the wind (see Isa. 26:18). Yet, as the coming awakening unfolds, the Holy Spirit will animate many that hunger and thirst for the fullness of the sons and daughters of God.

Let me describe to you in more detail this new order of end-time believer. They will have a strong sense of headship in Jesus Christ. They will resist the traditional pressures of religion that submits to the approval of men. They understand obedience and respect authority but recognize it is better to obey God than men. They are not rebels. There is no rebellion found in them. They are simply given over to the absolute word and will of God. They abandon all to follow Him. They are faithful in the least as well as the greatest things.

Such obedience comes out of extreme faith and confidence in the will of God as sovereign. Their faith is in God regardless of the circumstances. They have such confidence in the greater power of God at work in them, that whatever happens to them is regarded more as the sanctifying work of the Holy Spirit than as the destructive work of the enemy.

This company is nonreligious. They see the difference between religion and relationship. They do not need religion because they have a personal relationship with God. Religion means sacrifice; relationship means obedience. They are non-materialistic. They have learned with Paul to be content in whatever state they are. It does not matter whether they have or have not. Their confidence is in their God who provides. They think spirit, not flesh. They think eternal, not temporal.

Their experiences in the Spirit are not an end in themselves but a means for attaining the higher goal of Him. These are members of local churches without walls. They have gone outside the camp with Christ bearing His reproach. At times some churches become like walled cities keeping others unlike them out. God is not interested in building Christian social clubs or country clubs. Rather He is calling for a people to go out to gather them into His Kingdom.

The only wall that God is interested is the wall of fire in Zechariah 2:5. *"For I will be a wall of fire about her, and I will be the glory in her midst"* (NASB). They have taken on no honors, no names, and no recognition for themselves; they are nameless and faceless except in the name of Jesus shining on their face. They gather in no other name but His name. They follow no other name but His name. They hear no other voice but that of the Good Shepherd. They are joined to no one but to Him. They are bought at a price. They have no life to live but His life.

These are dead to their personal agenda, crucified in Him. They are true prophets of God since no man can buy them. They say what God says; they do what God does, and are what God has made them to be.

They're driving force and sole motivation is prompted by the leading of the Holy Spirit. They have living water flowing out of their bellies as rivers of life. They do not need to be prompted to praise and worship God. They do not need to be told to fast and pray. It is second nature to them. They listen to His voice within them, and are taught by His voice within them. They are born out of the fire, knowing persecution, but constantly seeing the blessings of God in pursuit of them. They are used to trials in life. They don't expect smooth sailing. They see the resistance of the devil but recognize the truth that God will prevail.

We notice that at times the world persecutes the traditional type of believer. It seems to mock the Spirit-led believer. The enemy will surely try to crucify the believer who presses into the Most Holy Place. Those that have a form of godliness but lack the power therein are no threat to the kingdom of darkness. Only overcomers who deny themselves and take up their cross daily threaten the enemy.

The devil trembles as the Holy Spirit prepares and calls forth these forged in the pattern of the Tabernacle. These will be a consuming fire for God. This, I believe, is the Church that Jesus is waiting to arise on the face of the earth—a people ravished by His heart, transformed by His Presence, compelled as Lions of the Tribe of Judah. John the Baptist, the first forerunner, pointed to the Lamb of God; this panoply of committed believers will point to the Lion of the Tribe of Judah. Jesus will return not as the Lamb but as the Lion.

Those who answer the call will be clothed in the power of the spirit of Elijah. The same portion that covered Elijah and John shall cover them. Elijah and John were clearly ones who entered into the fullness of the Tabernacle. They did not linger around the Outer Courts. They did not loiter at the curtain. They boldly entered into the throne room of grace. The new prototype of Elijah and John will be clothed in nothing but the power of God. They shall cast out demons and call down fire from the heavens. Signs, wonders, and miracles will follow them that believe. They will be baptized in repentance and baptized in fire. They will step out with God before them and behind them. The anointing they carry will not be the first portion, but the double portion. Like John, they will have the legal right to the double portion born out of Christ's pierced side. This new and awesome mantle will cover us in the endtimes and transform us in our inmost being. Like Jesus we will be Tabernacles among them as we pursue the fullness of the pattern of the Tabernacle.

CHAPTER THIRTEEN

THE CLOUD OF GLORY
(A CONSECRATED PEOPLE)

When the work on the Tabernacle was completed and everything was made in accordance to the specifications laid out by God, Moses then had each part put in its proper place. First, the tent cloth with its clasps, crossbars, posts, and bases were positioned. Then the various coverings and curtains of the Tabernacle were draped. Next, the Ark of the Covenant with its concealed items and the Mercy Seat were brought into the Holy of Holies.

Moses then called for the Table of the Showbread with its articles and bread, the pure Golden Lampstand with its lamps and oil for lighting, and the Golden Altar of Incense with its fragrant spices. Following the furnishings for the Holy Place was brought the Brazen Altar with its bronze gratings and all its utensils. Then, the Laver was brought in with its water. Finally, the curtains for around the courtyard along with its posts and bases were erected. Moses carefully examined the woven garments worn by the priests. All was prepared exactly as the Lord God directed.

Moses set up the Tabernacle exactly as the Lord God prescribed. The work was complete. He finally sprinkled all of it with blood and anointed it all with oil (see Exod. 40:33). What happened after the consecration of the Tabernacle was nothing short of miraculous. The word of God says that the cloud of glory, which settled on Mount Sinai when Moses went to meet with God, came and covered the Tabernacle.

Then the cloud covered the tabernacle of meeting, and the glory of the Lord filled the tabernacle. And Moses was not able to enter the tabernacle of meeting, because the cloud rested above it, and the glory of the Lord filled the tabernacle. (Exodus 40:34-35 NKJV).

God found the work of Moses pleasing to Him, so He rewarded Moses and the people with His abiding presence in the visible form of the cloud of His glory. When the cloud of His glory moved, so too the people of Israel would move following after the cloud. What this means to us is that God rewards a life consecrated and dedicated to Him. He promises to guide and direct our lives as we obediently live in Him. That His abiding presence changes us is also equally important. Let me explain this truth by way of illustration.

The Marinade

When I was a boy growing up I'd spend time with my mother in the kitchen. She was usually cooking and baking to feed nine hungry mouths. One of my favorite dinners she prepared was London broil, which we had on special occasions. I'd carefully watch mother as she scored the meat on both sides with a knife making shallow cuts. Then she placed the meat in a container of marinade made up of oil and many wonderful seasonings. The meat would sit in the marinade for several hours before it could be broiled. Being the impatient child that I was, I questioned mom as to why the meat had to marinade so long. She told me that was her secret to a delicious London broil. She explained that as the meat sat in the container, it took on the properties of the marinade. The marinade made the meat tender, juicy, and flavorful.

As we "marinate" in the presence of God, we take on the properties of God. His holiness, if you will, "rubs off" on us. This experience happened to Moses whenever he sat in the presence of God. The word of God says that Moses came down Mount Sinai after spending time in prayer with the Lord God. Moses received the Ten Commandments from the Lord, and *"he was not aware that his face was radiant because he had spoken with the Lord. When Aaron and all the Israelites saw Moses, his face was radiant, and they were afraid to come near him"* (Exod. 34:29-30). Sometimes Moses had to put a veil over his face to talk with the people. This radiance on the face of Moses is the presence of God lingering with him. By being in the manifested presence of God, Moses was changed. The more he sat in the presence of God, the more radiant Moses became.

The holiness of Moses and, de facto, *our* holiness does not arise from our moral and religious behavioral efforts.

The word *holiness* or *kabod* means a "separating from and a cutting off." Thus we can readily perceive the dividing or distinguishing of the secular from the profane. This dividing and separation implies a dividing and separation unto God's service. This dividing from the profane is not intended to make the individual extrinsically different looking from others as in the dress code of some religions. No. We are not talking about creating religious sects that dress differently. The differences we are pointing toward reflect the inner conviction and character of the God of revelation in the person of Jesus Christ. The word of God encourages us to *"put on the new man, which was created according to God in true righteousness and holiness"* (Eph. 4:24 NKJV).

Hans Kung in his monumental work *The Church* (Sheed and Ward, 1967) writes, "pure things become holy by being removed from their profane usage and dedicated to God."[xxii] The concept has a cultic background. The sense of separation is carried on in the New Testament. Here we find holy things set apart through the sanctifying will and word of God. The primary things set apart in the New Testament are the people of God chosen and sanctified by the Holy Spirit, who is the Spirit of holiness. His one work is the sanctification of humanity (see Rom. 1:4).

A Kingdom of Priests

God promised Moses that His people Israel would be *"a kingdom of priests and a holy nation"* (see Exod.19:6). That promise is to be fulfilled in the realization of our consecration as the Church to be *"a chosen people, a royal priesthood, a holy nation, a people belonging to God"* (1 Pet. 2:9).

Under the New Testament covenant, the good news is that no longer would only one man (Moses) go into the presence of God and come out with a veiled face. Under the New Covenant we all have access to the holy presence of the Most High God through the walk through the Tabernacle. No longer does one man dwell in the presence of God. *"For we who with unveiled faces all reflect the Lord's glory, are being transformed into His likeness with ever-increasing glory, which comes from the Lord, Who is the Spirit"* (2 Cor. 3:18). By relationship to God Most High the Holy Spirit transforms us personally and as a people. We are consecrated Tabernacles dwelling in the world. We are in the world but not of the world for we are set apart for His purposes. The Holy Spirit of God consecrates us as Jesus the Son of God was consecrated for the Father's purposes.

There is a wonderful, anecdotal story taken from the life of Smith Wigglesworth. In the year 1922, he was ministering as an evangelist in New Zealand. He called for a prayer meeting with 11 other leaders. While all were in prayer, the presence of God began to fill the room. Soon the glory of God became terrible. The light became too bright, the heat too intense. None of the other men could take it any longer. They had to leave the room. Only Smith Wigglesworth could continue in the midst of the Shekinah. He was caught up in the Spirit, radiant with holy fire[xxiii] (George Stormont, *Smith Wigglesworth: A Man who Walked with God*, Harrison House, 1989).

In our day, I believe many will be called forth to walk through the Tabernacle into the Shekinah presence of the Almighty. This call is not for the few but for many to answer. It will take a large number of consecrated people to carry the glory cloud into the world. The great cloud of witnesses who will walk through the Tabernacle and be consecrated to God will be ordinary people in one respect. They will be ordinary in the sense that they will be people like you and me. They will be extraordinary in the sense that they will be consecrated to God.

Have you ever spent time in the presence of someone you really enjoy? There is a little girl named Bethany in our home church that people simply love to be around. She is only 12 years old but has such a wonderful effect on people because of the presence of God she carries. God is raising up thousands like Bethany. The word *Bethany* means "house of figs or fruit." Bethany provided a place of hospitality for the Lord Jesus during His public ministry. The modern day "Bethanys" will provide places of hospitality for individuals in need of Jesus, and they will be known by their love one for another.

Thousands like Bethany will be like the high priest Joshua in the Book of Zechariah. The Lord God will say of them as He said of Joshua, *"Is not this man a burning stick snatched from the fire?"* (Zech. 3:2b). Joshua had walked through the fires of life before he was raised up. He was prepared for the ministry during his lifetime. Though the accuser of the brethren wanted to touch Joshua to do him harm, God intervened in behalf of his saint and rebuked satan. God then sent Joshua forth as a carrier of His divine presence in all the earth.

The result of this tactical planning will pay off for the Kingdom of God. Millions upon millions will be saved. Jews will call on the name of Yeshua. Muslims will see the power of miracles and come to Jesus in scores. Atheists and agnostics will cry out "Jesus is Lord." Satanists will affirm Jesus as Master. Sin will give way to the things of the Spirit, and His saving blood shed on the cross will make them free like never before.

Some have testimonies about how God touched their lives 10, 20, and 30 years ago. That was great for that time, but God is not back in the past. He is a God in the here and now. We need a fresh touch of His presence. Many will be revived when the Holy Spirit is poured out on all flesh. Visions and dreams and supernatural visitation will become common in those days: *"Your sons and daughters will prophesy, your old men will dream dreams, your young men will see visions. Even on my servants, both men and women, I will pour out My Spirit in those days"* (Joel 2:28-29).

We are on the edge of the greatest outpouring of the Spirit of God the world will ever see. We are living in a day of release when the power of God will be released as in the apostolic age. Reading the accounts from the Book of Acts still excites me. To know that this age of apostolic anointing is returning to the Church is even more exciting. The apostolic anointing will demand that we reevaluate our plans and strategies for our churches. It will cause our vision to grow beyond the borders and boundaries of what we now call church work. The Church may have to refocus to see in terms of Kingdom perspective rather than local church growth. By that I simply mean the focus may be more on city and community needs rather than on particular church needs. The real potential for evangelizing portions of the world will come from ordinary people like us, made extraordinary by God.

We will be commissioned and organized by God's Holy Spirit in strategies that will begin to evangelize the world in great ways for God. Many men, women, and children will walk through each and every station of the Tabernacle. They will gladly die to self-ambition. God will freely use us as carriers of His holy presence.

FINAL WORD

I see the Lord in His gracious heart preparing a Church to follow hard after Him. Not only will opportunities come to each, but also these opportunities will come at a time when the Church will experience the greatest move of God ever known. His call to follow Him goes out to all desiring to be consecrated in holiness. This call is for the creation of God's living Tabernacles to be carried throughout the earth. However, in God's economy of things, more important than anything we can do in ministry is just being in relationship with Him. His call is for a people to heed His unmistaken voice to follow Him.

In 1983 while in a spirit of prayer I sensed the Spirit of God put these words on my heart:

> *Draw close to Me, and I will draw close to you. Renew the joy of your salvation daily. Seek to get My word ever deeper into your heart. Empty yourself of the things of this world, and fill yourself with the things of God. I must come ahead of all others. Truth must come ahead of all else. Do not allow the justification of things, which God says are wrong. Do not call what God calls "good," not good. Do not call what God calls "not good," good. Take care not to allow yourself to be compromised. Beloved, I have called you into the light and truth. The blind cannot lead the blind. Pray without ceasing. Refuse to allow yourself to be worried. Stay alert, for you do not know the appointed time.*

It seems as though God wants above all else for us to use our time on earth to draw closer to His presence. It is as if nothing else matters as much to Him. He wants to empty us of the things of this world and fill us with the things that are eternal. We are to protect and guard our minds and our hearts. Not only that, but we are to renew them daily in the word of God. There is a sense of urgency in the tone of His words.

Like the Hound of Heaven, He pursues us to come follow Him. God is never satisfied with knowing us as an acquaintance, but rather wants us to make our life in a pursuit after Him. He provides a clear way for us to approach Him. First, God shows us the way to Him in the Tabernacle of Moses in the Old Covenant and then through Jesus in the New Covenant. God's sole passion is for souls. He is ever presenting Himself to us that we might find Him and go deeper with Him.

The Book of Joshua records that the Israelites receive their inheritance in the land of Canaan. God had given Moses instructions as to how to divide the land among the 12 tribes of Israel. Joshua assigned the allotments according to God's directive to Moses. Joshua did not assign a portion of the land to the tribe of Levites. This is significant. Did the Levites not receive a portion of their inheritance because they displeased God? No. The reason is quite the contrary. Remember, the Levites were the priestly tribe that pressed into the Holy of Holies. They above all the 12 tribes had a reverential respect and under-standing for the holy vessels of the Tabernacle. God delib-erately doesn't give them land but allows them to live in a wide array of towns and pastures in the Promised Land. God then simply tells the priests of the Lord Most High that, *"their priestly service of the Lord is their inheritance"* (Josh. 18:7). God then says something to them that is even more stunning. God says, *"I am your portion and your inher-itance…"* (Num. 18:20b). To pursue after the Lord God alone, to set Him above all other priorities in life, to wor-ship Him in His holy temple, is the call and portion of every member of the priesthood of all believers. Just as Jesus acknowledged Mary's prayer life above her sister Martha's housekeeping, God sees the ultimate purpose and reason for our life on earth being in relationship with Him. Being God's portion and inheritance makes us richer than all other people. By living in deep relationship with God, the Levites also became richer than all the kings of that time. They were never in a state of want or lack. They lived in abundance through the tithes and offerings of the other tribes. Whenever we make God our treasure, we possess all there is to possess.

EPILOGUE

John is referred to as "John the Revelator" because in the Book of Revelation he lays out a depiction of Jesus, an unveiling or manifestation of His divine nature (see Rev. 1:1). John's preeminent contribution as an expositor of the gospel is to highlight the divine nature of Jesus the Lord. Though he walked with Him, ate with Him, and spoke with Him as one who was fully human, his own eyes testified to the belief that Jesus is fully God, fully divine; the Word become flesh to tabernacle among us.

It is revelation that enabled John to make this leap of faith about Jesus. Revelation 1:2 clearly lays out that an angel made known this revelation to him about Jesus, and he simply testifies and bears witness to everything he saw. Romans 1:18 states that the truth about God is suppressed by the ungodly. It says that which is plainly seen from the beginning is imprinted upon humanity's consciences, but sin has blinded man to the self-evident fact that God is clearly discernible in all things in creation. This same spiritual blindness that hinders men from seeing God in the universe is the same spiritual blindness that hinders men from seeing God in Jesus. The imprint of God is within everyone, but the light must be "turned on" to see.

In the story of the healing of the man born blind in John's Gospel, it is not the physical sight to the blind man that is the greater miracle. It is not until Jesus confronts him with the question, "Do you believe in the Son of Man?" and he answers, "Who is He that I might believe?" that the man with the newly given sight "sees." Jesus replies to him, *"You are now seeing Him; He is the one speaking with you"* (see John 9:35-37). With this exchange the natural gives way to the supernatural; the Light overshadows all darkness. The revelation of the word manifests itself in opening the spirit of the man to see. What he hears from God transforms the man into a new creation who now can see.

This book, *Into His Presence*, is an attempt to take you on a journey which will forever change your ability "to see." By using the pattern of the Tabernacle given by God, we can "see" the Way to Him. We can follow the Truth like never before. We can live the Life we have always wanted. In short, you can go as deep as you want with God. There is always more of Him, and He will share with you. John followed a deep path into the presence of God, which led him to the glory of Jesus Christ. John lived for his eyes to see divine revelation. It is my prayer for you that you, like John, will have your eyes fully opened to see, perceive, and behold the divine revelation and glory of Jesus Christ.

REFERENCES

PART 1: STEPPING INTO GOD

[i] Tozer, A.W. *The Pursuit of God* (Christian Publications, 1993).

[ii] Tenney, Tommy. *The God Chasers* (Destiny Image, 1998).

[iii] Prince, Derek. *Atonement* (Chosen Books, 2000).

[iv] DSM-IV category of Personality Disorders.

[v] Kernberg, Otto. Borderline *Conditions and Pathological Narcissism* (Jason Aronson, 1975).

[vi] Lewis , C. S. *The Four Loves* (Harcourt, Brace and Co., 1960).

[vii] Gershen Kaufman.

[viii] Bevere, John. *The Bait of Satan* (Creation House, 1994).

PART 2: STEPPING INTO POWER

[ix] Murray, Andrew. in his classic work, *The Holiest of All* (Whitaker House, 1997).

[x] Chevreau, Guy. *Pray with Fire* (Harper Collins, 1995).

[xi] Wessel, Helen. *Charles G. Finney* (Bethany House, 1977).

[xii] Bronowski, Jacob. *Ascent of Man* (Little, Brown, and Company, 1973).

[xiii] Goll, James. *Father Forgive Us* (Destiny Image, 1999).

PART 3: STEPPING INTO PASSION

[xiv] Spurgeon, C.M. *The Early Years* ().

[xv] Murray, Andrew. *The Holiest of All* (Whitaker House, 1996).

[xvi] Manning, Brennan. *Lion and Lamb* (Chosen Books, 1986).

[xvii] Conner, Kevin. *The Tabernacle of Moses* (City Bible Publishing, 1976).

[xviii] Bickly, Mike. *Passion for Jesus*.

[xix] "Friends of the Bridegroom." Poetry by Gary Wiens.

[xx] (*Revell's Bible Dictionary* 1990).

[xxi] Fletcher, John. *The Life of Smith Wigglesworth* (Ann Arbor:Vine Publications, 1988).

[xxii] Kung, Hans *The Church* (Sheed and Ward, 1967).

[xxiii] Stormont, George.